W9-CPE-358

THE JOKE-TELLER'S HANDBOOK

the Joke-Teller's Handbook

or

1,999 BELLY LAUGHS

BY ROBERT ORBEN

Bell Publishing Company • New York

INTRODUCTION

You will find this to be a different type of humor book. Such efforts are usually made up of anecdotes and rather lengthy stories. THE JOKE-TELLER'S HANDBOOK, in comparison, concentrates on the short, sharp, modern form of comedy explosion known as the "one-liner." A one-line joke is not necessarily one sentence in length; it may run two, three or more. The distinquishing factor is the use of as few words as possible to set up the comic situation and deliver the laugh via a punch line or phrase.

The one-line variety of comedy is the basis for most modern humor, yet surprisingly little of it has found its way into hard cover books. When it has, the accent has been on bon mots and clever sayings that lean on wit, instead of fun for fun's sake. This line of demarcation between wit and comedy is a critical one. Wit achieves intellectual approval and, perhaps, a smile. Comedy tickles the funny bone and brings forth the belly laugh.

The purpose of this book is to provide a stockpile of bright, laugh-loaded one-liners that can be put to a multitude of uses. In a world where "image" takes on ever increasing importance, humor is one of the best devices to create rapport and a friendly basis of understanding between individuals and groups. Laughs are vital to the effectiveness of speeches, sales presentations, lectures, instruction, and other forms of communication. Social success is largely dependent on the entertainment level of our conversation. The apt inclusion of humor is always welcome.

Let's talk a little about the "how" of getting laughs. The application of humor falls into two general categories: directed and non-directed. I call it Directed Comedy when you have a humorous talk or performance to give and you deliberately set about to add specific jokes to the presentation. Non-directed humor is spontaneous humor which often masquerades under the misnomer of ad-libbing. Study and observation will soon convince you that the best ad-libbers are those people who have encyclopedic joke memories and instantaneous recall of the right line for the right situation.

This prepared ad-libbing is a skill that can be developed. All that it requires is a sustained effort to read a few dozen jokes a day. You need not attempt to memorize them. Start with this book and plan to read ten pages a day, as you would a novel. Go through it once and then start all over again. By the time you will have read it four or five times, several hundred one-liners will be a part of your humor unconscious, ready to be called into play at a straight-line's notice!

Directed comedy requires a little more discipline. If you are a non-professional performer and want to add a dash of laughter to a speech, read it through and determine the key subjects covered. Then turn to the categories in this book that are on the subjects or allied to them. You will quickly find lines and comedy thoughts that can be spliced into the talk with little or no adaptation.

If your intention is to present a completely comic speech (a monologue, as it is known professionally) choose the theme or premise on which the jokes will be based. Let's assume you are going to poke some fun at television. Turn to the category labeled Television and read through the one-liners found there. In so doing, look for a story line or springboard thought to which the individual jokes will be applied. Modern comedy requires a point of view, an attitude. A successful comedy monologue must take a stand on a subject, and the specific gags are laugh points along the way.

A possible premise might be the perennial popularity of TV Westerns. Take all the jokes about TV Westerns from the Television category and copy them onto slips of paper or three by five cards. You can now rearrange them until you have established a continuity between the laughs and a reasonably smooth blending of one joke into another. It is wise to limit yourself to seven or eight jokes on a single premise and then go on to another subject. Each one of these sequences is commonly referred to as a "chunk" and three or four such "chunks", put together, make an acceptable ten-minute comedy act.

Much has been said and written about "timing" in the delivery of comedy material. This advice has rarely been of help to the timid or novice comedy performer. "Timing" boils down to this: there is a right and a wrong way to deliver comedy material, but what is right for one person is dead wrong for another. The same joke, with minor variations of expression, emphasis, and wording, can fit widely differing comic attitudes. You have to determine the approach to humor that works for you—and the only way to do this effectively is by trial and error.

Don't try to recite comedy material. Put the jokes in your own words while maintaining the basic structure of the gag. Always try to keep the key word or phrase at the very end of the one-liner so that the comic intent comes as a surprise. As this is written, conversational humor is the fad. Therefore, you can impart a quasi-believability to your material by relating it to real people, places and events. Above all, try to add a fun feeling to your delivery and look on the audience as a warm party of friends instead of a cold, menacing maw.

Comedy is fun, and there is a heady exhilaration in hearing the laughter and applause that follows a well-timed, neatly executed piece of humor. So, enough of theorizing—on to the belly laughs! I envy you your first encore!

BOB ORBEN

CONTENTS

CONTENTS

M

N

O

P

R

S

ADVERTISING

A

I think there's a lot more truthfulness in advertising than there used to be. Two weeks ago I bought one of those collapsible swimming pools for the kids. This morning it did.

I was just thumbing through a magazine and they had a big ad in there reading ECZEMA! Isn't it remarkable the things they're selling these days?

It doesn't make sense—like a falsie manufacturer advertising: "Beware of imitations!"

We bought a bed and we bought it from a very reliable company. Their motto is: "WE STAND BEHIND EVERY BED WE SELL!" I just hope they don't peek.

Don't wait until it's too late! Write your Congressman today. Demand they stop defacing our billboards with highways!

Did you see that wonderful ad in one of the show business papers last week? LION TAMER—WANTS TAMER LION.

Everybody goofs once in a while. Just last week a big department store ran a full page ad with the headline: MATERNITY DRESSES— FOR THE MODERN MISS!

Nowadays a Western has to have an unusual twist. Like the one about the Madison Avenue ad exec who went out to Arizona and became a cowboy. Through the years he worked and slaved to make people think he was born in the saddle—but one thing always gave him away. Instead of saddlebags, he carried two attaché cases . . . and gray flannel chaps. . . .

I love the one about the Kansas City feed manufacturer who brought in a Madison Avenue copywriter to hypo business. How else could they have gotten the slogan: OUR PIG MASH IS GOOD TO THE LAST SLOP!

And now we bring you a ten-second horror story. It's a classified ad in this morning's paper under FOR SALE. Reads: 1926 Stutz Bearcat. Take over payments.

AGENTS

If I had it to do over again, I'd be an agent. These are boys who've got it made. I've got an agent who gets 10% of everything I get—except my ulcers.

Actually, I was supposed to open here six months ago—but my idiot agent booked me for a one-nighter in Alaska.

I was talking to my agent this morning. You know what an agent is—sort of a Mack the Knife who does it with contracts.

I'm not one of those comics who always knock their agent. Why I even give 10% of my unemployment checks to my agent. Let's face it—I figure he's responsible for them.

AIR-CONDITIONING

I think air-conditioning is wonderful. Now you don't have to wait till December to get a cold. You can have one all year round.

The management spared no expense to make our stay a comfortable one. They even air-conditioned the steam room.

I want to apologize for the heat in here. We had a very unusual breakdown of our air-conditioning system. What makes it so unusual—it hasn't been delivered yet! . . . It broke down on a truck outside Albuquerque, New Mexico. . . . We may be sweltering in here—but those drivers on Route 66—cool, man, cool! . . .

This is such a small, intimate, friendly group—why don't we do something different tonight—like going out to watch the air-conditioner break down?

Personally, I think those air-conditioners are mechanical psychologists. Have you ever noticed they never break down when the temperature is 70? But the minute it passes 90—boinnnnnng! I won't say we've been having trouble with the air-conditioning but I'll bet we are the only place in town with a sleep-in repairman. . . . And it's on a very unusual basis. He only gets paid for the time it's working. So far, since June, he's made $13. . . .

But air-conditioning is a wonderful thing. Remember the good old days—when air-conditioning was an oscillating fan behind a cake of ice? . . . And how far we've progressed? Now people can't work in the summertime unless their teeth are chattering. . . .

Civilization can bring about some pretty crazy things. I know a guy who leaves his air-conditioned office at five, climbs into his air-conditioned Cadillac and drives to his air-conditioned club—so he can take a steam bath!

AIR FORCE

And those jet planes—1,000 miles an hour! 1,500 miles an hour! 2,000 miles an hour! Things are moving so fast, I hear the Air Force is junking 600 brand new fighters. They're obsolete. You can see them!

The draft board wanted to put me in the Air Force. The Air Force! I get dizzy when my barber pumps the chair too high!

I'm telling you, those Air Force boys never let up. Now they're working on something that's really top secret—a sound that can travel faster than planes!

ALASKA

As the Honorable Senator from Texas once put it: (TEXAS TWANG) "When those Eskimos convinced Congress to make Alaska the

49th State, the American people got the biggest snow job in history!"

There's still fortunes to be made if you use your imagination! I know a guy who went up to Alaska and he's got it made—sells unfrozen food!

I just heard of an Alaskan who wants to visit Texas but he's afraid to. Suffers from claustrophobia.

Most Texans don't exactly believe in Heaven and Hell. When they die, they figure they either go to Dallas or Alaska.

I think Texans have a right to get mad about Alaska. I mean, they've taken the jokes all right. They've accepted the fact that Texas is now the second largest state. It's those CARE packages from Fairbanks—that's what hurts!

You don't know what it means to a Texan to hear people telling rich Alaskan jokes!

You know what I think hurts Texans the most? The thought that if we ever split Alaska in two—Texas'd be the *third* largest state.

I still say Texas is bigger than Alaska. Let's face it, if you compare highballs—you don't count the ice.

I won't say the transit system in Nome is primitive, but it's the first time I ever saw a cross-town bus that barked.

You know what's fun? Playing golf in Alaska! You hit a ball down the fairway—and by the time it stops rolling, it's four feet wide!

Talk about kicking a man when he's down—I just read about a Fairbanks cocktail lounge that offers Alaskan martinis for 75¢— Texas size: 50¢!

You don't realize what prosperity is doing to Alaska. The Eskimos still drive sleds but they're not pulled by dogs any more—eight Volkswagens!

Alaskan cities are growing so fast, they're beginning to have traffic problems. Just last week, Dawson City put up its first traffic signal. It says: MUSH—DON'T MUSH!

They say the days in Alaska are six months long. Can you imagine? Six months long! What a place to sell No Doz!

Then there's the one about the gold-rich sourdough who bought a sled for $80,000. It's a little different from most sleds. Instead of dogs, it's pulled by ten Cadillacs.

ANXIETY

Nervous? This boy is half-man; half-Miltown.

Wouldn't that be a wonderful name for a tranquilizer—Damnitol?

Personally, I felt a lot more safe and secure back in 1933, when all I had to fear was fear itself.

I just had a wonderful dream. I dreamed the Joneses were trying to keep up with me!

But you don't really know the meaning of the word anxiety unless you're a sports car owner entirely surrounded by tall dogs!

I won't say what condition my nerves are in—but I have to take two shots of bourbon just to quiet me down enough so I can open my bottle of Miltowns.

Nervous? If the butterflies in my stomach ever got together, they could carry me right outta here.

I know a guy who's a real sadist. It just so happens that his best friend is a hypochondriac—and all day long he keeps telling him how well he looks.

This girl takes so many tranquilizers—if she breathes at you, you go limp.

The way things are going, you feel like a fool buying a five-year calendar.

It's a wonderful idea—Miltown cheese dip for people who want to give quiet parties.

I may look healthy, but under all this tan, you should know how pale I am!

It gets you all shook up—like trying to decide which checkout line at the supermarket to stand on.

What's the matter with you? You're as nervous as a clam at low tide.

Now they've got a tranquilizer atomizer. One spray and it calms you down to the point where you can take a pill.

You think you've got troubles? What about the neurotic who thinks his inferiority complex is bigger and better than anybody else's in the world?

It's all right to have problems, but this kid is a Freudian Smorgasbord.

I won't say he's neurotic—but last week he was watching the Army-Navy game on television—and every time one of the teams went into a huddle—he wondered if they were talking about *him.*

They're just one of those incompatible couples. He's on Miltown and she's on Benzedrine.

I feel good today. Wingin'! Like you do on those rare days when your pep pills get a little ahead of your tranquilizers!

APARTMENTS

I was reading one of those PREVIEWS OF 1975 articles, and they claim by 1975 they'll be able to heat an entire apartment building with one lump of coal! By 1975? I've got a landlord who's trying to do it now!

She said she had a lush apartment. I didn't believe it until I tripped over a drunk.

He calls it his penthouse in the sky. His girl friends say it's more of a take-you-apartment.

Talk about co-operation! We've got a janitor in our apartment house who'll do anything to make us feel comfortable. This morning the temperature in the living room was 50 degrees. He came right up and helped me bang on the radiator.

ARMY

I know a fella who was drafted; was sent to Fort Dix; and that afternoon was made a Brigadier General. It's kinda thrilling the way he describes it. He's standing on this line, naked, with an IBM card in his hand, much too small to do any good . . . when he drops it and a guy with golf shoes walks across it. . . .

Every Armed Forces Day my thoughts go back to the recent difference of opinion people are calling World War II. . . . Personally, I don't like that title at all. Sounds like it's one of a series —to be continued. . . .

You can always tell a World War II veteran. He's the one who will never be able to refer to it as creamed chipped beef on toast.

I just tried on my old Army uniform and the only thing that fits is the tie.

I can still remember those wonderful Army doctors. One day we were having war games and a fella staggered in gasping: "Doc! Doc! I've been gassed!" And Kildare answered: "Easy, son, the bicarbonate'll be here in a minute!"

The drill sergeant was looking at his platoon of recruits—his face a study in disgust. "Look at yuz! Ya hair ain't combed; ya uniforms ain't pressed; ya lines are all crooked! Suppose Russia suddenly declared war?"

Sometimes I wonder about West Point. Are they building an army capable of licking Russia—or Notre Dame?

You know what the Pentagon is. That's a big building in Washington that has five sides—on almost every issue.

Did you see that Army drill sergeant who's riding around with special license plates: HUP 234?

Our impression of a GI in West Berlin saying goodnight to his date:
GI: How about giving me your phone number, Baby?
G. Liebchen 9-9999.
GI: All right, then. Don't!

ASTRONAUTS

I just had a horrible thought. What if we're paying those astronauts by the mile?

I don't care what you say, these astronauts are just like any other tourists. All they ever do is talk about their trip.

There used to be more astronauts but one of them was disqualified for morale reasons. The one named Icarus.

Do you think those astronauts ever forget where they are and call for the stewardess?

It's kind of a shame the way those astronauts have put everybody else down. Last week the circus shot a man from a cannon—and six people yawned.

One of those astronauts is giving the scientists an awful hard time. When the weather's nice—he wants to ride with the top down.

ATOMIC ENERGY

In case of atomic attack, don't panic. Go down to your local finance company; take out a $25,000 loan; then relax. They'll make darn sure nothing happens to you!

Nowadays, you wanna be the most popular guy on the block—you don't have to brush your teeth with the right toothpaste; own color TV; or take frug lessons. Just build your own bomb-shelter —with a guest room.

You know, with all this talk about A-bombs that'll destroy a city; H-bombs that'll destroy a state; and chain reactions that'll destroy a world—you just don't have any incentive to buy a two pants suit.

It's good to read Dear Abby now and then. What with Russia and Red China and the H-bomb—it's wonderful to know there are still some people in this world whose biggest worry is how they should acknowledge a wedding present.

I wanna show you people how much radioactivity there *is* in the air (HOLD UP ONE OF THE SELF-LIGHTING BULBS SOLD IN NOVELTY SHOPS).

What with atom bombs, H-bombs, intercontinental ballistic missiles—I tell you, I'm not even saving Green Stamps any more.

You know what worries me? If they keep fooling around with H-bombs—someday they're gonna pick a Miss Universe—and there won't be any Universe left to be Miss of.

This fallout scare is really lousing up those health instructors on TV. They're saying: "Altogether now—breathe deep!" And nobody'll do it.

It's a shame generations hundreds of years from now can't be here to watch these atom bomb tests. Just so they'll know why they look so funny.

Things haven't changed much. You still run into ambitious people who want to set the world on fire—only now we call them nuclear physicists.

B

BACHELORS

BACHELOR PARTY: I understand there's a young fella with us to-night who's gonna get married next week (MAKE HIM STAND UP, AND LEAD THE APPLAUSE). Well, I think that's wonderful. In fact, I'd like to give you two bits of advice my father gave to me. First —always maintain the right to spend one night each week with the boys. And the second bit of advice—don't waste it on the boys!

B: I got a wonderful idea! Why don't you come up to my apartment; we'll have a quiet little supper by candlelight; play a few records; then around midnight we'll open a bottle of champagne and toast the New Year!
G: But the New Year is five months away.
B: You don't have to leave early, do you?

Did you read that news story claiming one out of every six British men is a homosexual? Makes you wonder how there'll always be an England.

Which brings us to a parting thought for all bachelors: 'Tis better to have loved and lost—think of all the PTA and Little League meetings you're missing.

BANKS

Did you ever get the feeling that a bank is a large impressive institution where you keep the government's money until April 15th?

This is dedicated to the tellers at the First National Bank—five people who really know what I've gone through.

So this Italian immigrant walks into a Fifth Avenue bank and

27

says: "Pardona mia—I'd like to talk with the fella what arranges loans." The guard replies: "I'm sorry, but the loan arranger is out to lunch." "In data case, I talk to Tonto!"

COLD CASH: what they keep in air-conditioned banks.

You gotta be ingenious. I know a guy who borrowed $5,000—spent the last six months opening new bank accounts. Got clocks, radios, luggage, dishes—gave the $5,000 back; opened his own discount house.

It doesn't make sense—like opening a Savings Bank in Las Vegas.

The bank just asked me to join their Christmas Club. Frankly, there's only one thing holding me back—the dues.

I just joined a new kind of Christmas Club. Every week you put a little money into the bank—and before you know it you've saved enough to pay for *last* year's gifts.

You think you got troubles. The bank just threw me out of their Christmas Club. Claimed I wasn't coming to meetings!

With the world on the brink of disaster, isn't it wonderful the way people are helping one another? Like all these bank mergers—think how many hours it's gonna save hold-up men.

BASEBALL

What's all this excitement about baseball again? I thought they decided who the champions were last Fall?

The baseball season's starting up and one team's really going in for training. Just hired four coaches—one for hitting, one for fielding, one for pitching, and one for Gillette commercials.

Talk about predicaments—there's this Little Leaguer with a real problem. The Coach orders him to hold up at third—and his mother is yelling: "Come home this instant!"

Well here it is August—the month in which the Yankees usually print up their World Series tickets.

I just had a crazy thought. Do you think they'd ever call a night game on account of daylight?

Talk about summer replacements—the biggest one seems to be first place in the major leagues.

You gotta admit the ——————— have a great team this year. They've got at least two pitchers who can throw no-hitters—and four fielders who can throw entire games.

Did you ever have one of those days when everything seems to go wrong? Like the ballplayer who's hitting .196; strikes out three times in a row; commits two errors—then goes down to do a shaving commercial and cuts himself.

Personally, I don't care who wins the World Series providing the (PICK ONE OF THE TEAMS) don't lose.

I know a pitcher who made over $100,000 last year—lost nine games out of eleven, hit .067, but he does a helluva Gillette commercial!

It's a funny thing. I always thought baseball was the national pastime. Then I subscribed to PLAYBOY.

You think you've got troubles! I know a ballplayer who's in the worst slump of his career; the team is sending him back to the Minors—and if that isn't enough—Gillette is taking its razor back!

I was just reading about a ballplayer who was in such a bad slump—he did a TV shaving commercial, took a swipe at his face —and missed!

Remember the good old days, when baseball players shaved at home instead of on television?

BEATNIKS

Isn't that a wonderful name they've given to these characters with long, shaggy hair; dirty sweat shirts; shapeless dungarees and sneakers? They call them Beatniks—and just three years ago we would have called them slobs. I mean, that's progress!

There's one thing about being a Beatnik. You're never gonna miss an important phone call cause you're in the shower.

Some of these Beatniks are mighty confused people. I know one who's a masochist. Takes baths.

Did you hear the one about the Beatnik maid? Every day she comes in and dirties up a bit.

How bout those Beatniks? I saw one the other day—dirty sweat shirt, jeans, long dirty hair, a beard—I mean, she looked awful!

All the Beatniks are wearing goatees. Gives them that Fidel Castro after taxes look.

But that's the big thing now—beards. It's a symbol of all those revolting against society. Revolting—I guess that's what you'd call it.

BEATNIKS: people who express their dislike for conformity by dressing, talking and smelling alike.

I never thought I'd see the day when there'd be more blue jeans on Broadway than in Kansas.

Have you read that new Beatnik Cookbook? Talk about wild recipes, one calls for lettuce and tomatoes—then you add a dash of marijuana and the salad tosses itself!

I know one Beatnik poet who was exiled to Staten Island. Someone found out his last poem rhymed.

Talk about crazy ideas—did you hear about this Beatnik Western they're making? The hero doesn't roll cigarettes—he rolls drunks!

Beatniks are making a big thing of Christmas. They figure Santa Claus is one of them—since he doesn't shave and only works one day a year.

BEAUTY CONTESTS

My impression of a beauty contest winner who's GOT to make it in Hollywood: (PRETEND YOU'RE USING A TAPE MEASURE) Hmmmm.

Let's see now—39 inches! Very good! And now we'll measure the other one.

Talk about sensational tape recordings—how about those made from the Miss Universe entries?

One of the Miss Universe contestants was so shook up by all the excitement, she went into a drugstore, ordered a tube of toothpaste, the clerk asked her what size—she answered 40-25-36.

BOOKS

How times have changed. Just 20 years ago most of the best seller list would have been mailed in plain white wrappers.

I'm writing a book that's gonna have the field all to itself. It's for people who want to be unpopular, unadjusted, unsuccessful and fat!

You gotta be shrewd to make it nowadays. For instance, I know a fella who's lolling in loot. Put out REBECCA OF SUNNYBROOK FARM as a paperback—but right across the front it said: UNEXPURGATED!

It's the heartrending story of a girl who doesn't have any boy friends 'cause she's only 16—where she should be 38.

You gotta be more tolerant of people. If you stop to think about it, you spent hours and hours of your childhood reading about the most famous Junkie of them all—Sherlock Holmes! One of his best-known expressions was: "Quick Watson, the needle!" And that boy didn't own a hi-fi!

C: It's so infuriating—like reading a murder mystery in Chinese.
S: What's so infuriating about reading a murder mystery in Chinese?
C: You get to know the murderer on the very first page.

It's the story of a very shy Italian girl who's never been pinched before. Only behind.

I hear they're putting out a New Hampshire edition of LADY CHATTERLEY'S LOVER. Calling it: LADY CHATTERLEY'S T'OTHER.

I don't mind my wife reading things like LADY CHATTERLEY'S LOVER—but yesterday she brought home a game-keeper . . . I mean, do you blame me for being suspicious? All we've got is one lousy Monopoly set! . . .

I won't say she spends all her time reading—but we've got a boy eight years old and he only knows one word: "Shhhhhhh!"

I don't do much reading. In fact, the last book I read was THE HIDDEN PERSUADERS. And I only read that by accident. Thought it was about Jayne Mansfield.

I'll bet I'm one of the few people in America who hasn't read FANNY HILL. Not that I don't want to. I'm just waiting for the illustrated edition.

BOOK TITLES

I WAS A TEENAGE ELDER STATESMAN

LIVE ALONE AND LACK IT

WHAT MAKES WYATT EARP?

HOW TO AVOID AN EMOTIONAL CRISIS WHILE SELECTING FRENCH PASTRY

GOODBYE, MAMA, I'M OFF TO CINERAMA

A HANDY BOOK OF REMINDERS FOR FORGETFUL ELEPHANTS

HOW TO RETIRE AT THE AGE OF 12

HOW TO ACHIEVE FINANCIAL INDEPENDENCE THROUGH PROPER BUDGETING by Barbara Hutton

101 RISQUE STORIES by Salvatore Risque

BOWLING

Did you hear the one about the ministers who formed a bowling team? Called themselves the Holy Rollers?

I won't say he cheats, but he won't go bowling any more. Who can tilt an alley?

Talk about Puritans—I once knew a girl who wouldn't even go bowling. Claimed if you had to play it in an alley, it couldn't be respectable.

BROADWAY

What excitement on Broadway this morning! A new show ran an ad for chorus boys and over 60 odd fellas showed up.

I won't say what the play was like—but the prompter got three curtain calls.

Next week we're doing a dramatization of the first 800 pages of Tolstoy's great novel—WAR AND PEACE. . . . I'm playing War and we're casting the other roles from the chorus. . . . It's a story of conflict, pillage, lust and bestiality—with a few chuckles thrown in for the locals. . . . Children under 16 will not be admitted unless accompanied by their husbands. . . .

You might say the show got divided notices. We liked it but the critics didn't.

I hear they're gonna revive LEND AN EAR again. LEND AN EAR— wouldn't that be a wonderful title for the life of Van Gogh?

BUSINESS

Let's face it, the American businessman is in a tight spot. Whenever he comes up with something new—the Russians invent it a month later and the Japanese make it cheaper!

The drug industry is so concerned over investigations, it's overlooking the greatest danger of them all. Some day all those millions of decay bacteria are gonna rise up and destroy all that toothpaste!

Then I opened a lingerie shop and became King of the Undieworld.

I know a chorus girl who's got her own way of knowing when there's a recession. That's when she doesn't feel the pinch.

He's so proud 'cause through the entire recession, he was able to keep his head above water. Of course! Wood floats!

Everybody says the recession is over. So how come the boss called up the Better Business Bureau this morning? Asked them to send one over.

I didn't believe there was a recession until last week—when I saw this Texan buying a Volkswagen on time.

I'm mad at the whole textile industry! Can you imagine—making dish towels marked HIS and HERS!

An elderly executive retired, went to Persia, and bought himself a harem. Can you imagine that? The poor guy is having delusions of glandeur.

I won't say I'm a lousy businessman, but you're looking at the only guy who ever went bankrupt during the busy season.

IBM just unveiled a machine that does the work of a thousand men. They say it can actually think! Not if it does the work of a thousand men, it can't.

C

CARS

You can tell that Spring is here—all the used car lots are in bloom. I went to one yesterday and you should have seen this salesman. He started off by calling the car a giveaway—and in less than sixty seconds he accelerated the price to $1,400. . . . He had one car that was really a buy. One owner—a little old lady bank robber who only used it for getaways. . . .

The new cars are coming out this month. Now's your chance to get a look at what you'll be dodging all next year.

I hear Detroit is working on its biggest innovation in years. A windshield wiper that won't hold parking tickets!

Someone just identified the loudest noise known to man—the first rattle in your new car.

And did you notice the fronts of the new cars? Personally, I don't think they're grilles at all. Look more like pedestrian strainers.

This car is so advanced, the dashboard doesn't have buttons—zippers!

I understand Detroit is bringing out a new car specifically built for big city traffic. It's called a stationary wagon.

These modern cars are terrific! They'll get you anywhere. No matter where you go, they'll get you.

Talk about a switch, I just read of a new car dealer who raffled off a church!

Remember when you only had three considerations in buying a car? Price, color and make? Now you have to worry about nationality as well.

I like that new French car built along feminine lines. Everything's

35

different. You don't put gas in a tank any more—you just dab a little behind each headlight. . . . And it's just loaded with features that appeal to women! Lavender-wall tires . . . a low-cut grille . . . and padded bumpers, you'll love it! . . . They brought one into Detroit and three Ramblers chased it into an alley! . . .

Did you notice that item about Picasso being bumped by a hit and run driver in France? The police asked Picasso to draw a sketch of the driver and the very next day they arrested three suspects—a nun, the Eiffel Tower, and a TV set.

Did you see that new Japanese car? Smoooooth! And those slanted headlights—crazy, man, crazy! . . . But I understand they're very powerful. In fact, they've got *four* forward speeds—1st, 2nd, 3rd, and Banzai! . . .

I just read a startling statistic. There are 84,000,000 car radios in the United States today. What makes it so startling—there are only 64,000,000 cars!

I guess you heard about the fella who invented an electric car. For three dollars' worth of electricity you can drive it from Los Angeles to New York. There's only one hitch—that $5,000 extension cord.

Would the person who owns the Cadillac convertible with the cowhide seatcovers, please report to the parking lot? There's a bull attacking the back seat.

What a car! I'm gonna call it Flattery 'cause it gets me nowhere!

I wouldn't call it expensive. Let's just say it's the kind of car that can keep you strapped without safety belts.

I won't say the car is old but it's the first time I ever saw bifocal headlights.

I won't say what it looks like, but the last time I brought it into a garage—they suggested I keep the oil and change the car.

Did you ever stop to think—if all the cars in this country were laid end to end—it'd be Labor Day?

Isn't this a wonderful world we're living in? Take automobiles. Here it's still '66 and we're already seeing the '67s we'll be paying for in '68, '69 and '70.

I won't say the railroads are in trouble—but what do you wanna bet, come 1970, this country'll have 8,000,000 station wagons and no stations!

CHARITY

December—when every mail brings at least three appeals for money. I dunno. Remember the good old days—when charity was a virtue instead of an industry?

They're always saying that women are more charitable than men but that's not so. Why a tramp came up to me last night and I was extremely generous. And so was she!

Next week we're holding a 14-hour telethon for the worthiest cause of them all. We're gonna raise money to stamp out telethons!

It's just wonderful, the generosity of Americans. I know one outfit that's already collected $3,000,000—and they don't even have a disease yet!

Talk about easy jobs, how about the guy who runs the 100 Neediest Cases in Beverly Hills?

CHILDREN

Kids are so sophisticated these days. I saw three of them playing on the street with guns this morning. The first kid was a Space Cadet. The second said he was a Martian Bandit. And the third? What else? A UN mediator!

Everything's changing. Remember when kids asked you to tuck them in at night? Now they've all got electric blankets. You have to plug them in!

I can remember when kids used to run away. Now they defect.

He's the studious, horn-rimmed glasses type. The kind of a kid who worries about the shortage of teachers.

Kids are getting so cynical these days. I know one in Dallas who doesn't even believe in John Wayne.

So this little kid from Sutton Place gets a space suit and an atomic ray gun for his birthday. So excited, he runs out to where his friends are playing cowboys and Indians. One of them points a six-shooter at him and yells: "Bang! Bang! You're dead!" He points the ray gun right back and says: "Zap! Zap! You're sterile!"

I like the one about the kid with the horn-rimmed glasses who's getting a terrific tongue-lashing from his mother for using a four-letter word. "But, Mother," he interrupts, "Tennessee Williams uses that word all the time." And the good woman answers: "Well, don't play with him then!"

We've been letting our six-year-old go to sleep listening to the radio and I'm beginning to wonder if it's a good idea. Last night he said his prayers. Wound up with: "And God bless Mommy and Daddy and Sister. Amen—and FM!"

It's fascinating how kids get things balled up. I know one Sunday School teacher who listened real close and heard a five-year-old singing it: "Round John Virgin."

A little Mexican boy was told to write the first stanza of The Star-Spangled Banner, so he began: "Jose, can you see?"

And have you ever listened to some of the dialogues these kids come up with? He says: "Kiss me!" and she says: "No." He says: "Kiss me!" She says: "Noooo!" He says: "Kiss me and I'll split a Good Humor with ya!" "Awright!"

Then there's the ten-year-old who came out of his first Carroll

Baker movie saying: "As far as I'm concerned, Matt Dillon has had it!"

Then there's the ten-year-old with problems. She wants to know when she'll be old enough to not wear lipstick like the rest of the girls.

I was kind of a shy little kid. All I wanted to do was marry the girl next door—which was rather astute of me, 'cause next door was Minsky's.

Have you ever spent a Saturday afternoon baby-sitting? Believe me, somebody could make a fortune giving tired blood transfusions to six-year-olds!

I'll say this about my kids—at least we taught them how to share —measles, mumps, chicken pox.

Dirty? After this kid takes a bath, we don't know whether to clean the tub or dredge it.

My little daughter's only two and she knows just what she wants for Christmas—a baby sister. What can I say? Let's face it, there just aren't enough shopping days left!

Kids—you gotta follow the straight and narrow path—like you was shopping in the supermarket!

196_ happens to be the __th Anniversary of the founding of the Boy Scouts—and I just had a very sad thought. Can't you just see that first Boy Scout, somewhere, being helped across a street?

The kids came home from camp today and it was wonderful. One of them brought back a hand-carved ash tray that only cost me $800. . . . Around the edge it reads SOUVENIR OF CAMP SHAWANOHOPATONGOLAPI. Took him an hour to make the ash tray and eight weeks to do the lettering

Sometimes I wish they wouldn't make kids write home from camp. Yesterday I got a one-page note—blue crayon on a field of yellow chicken fat. . . . He didn't have too much to say, but what a zinger of a finish: "And by the way, Pop, how do you spell tuberculosis?" . . .

Personally, I didn't mind having the kids home all summer. Gave them some light little chores to do about the house and it worked out very well—although the three-year-old did have a little trouble putting on the new roof. . . . I don't know what I'm gonna do with that boy. Three years old and all he does is read science fiction stories. Things about a cow jumping over the moon—someone called Chicken Little predicting the end of the world. . . .

Have you noticed how many more twins are being born than ever before? I think the kids are getting afraid to come into this world alone.

CHRISTMAS

Well here it is Christmas again—the time of holly wreaths, mistletoe, pine trees, carols, eggnog—and Tin Pan Alley has even added a reverent touch with THE SILENT NIGHT WATUSI.

I love that wonderful old carol: GOOD KING WENCES—the one you have to sing with your lips closed.

It's so embarrassing, getting drunk on eggnog. What can you say to people—you're under the influence of cinnamon?

I hear there's an undercover group called Atheists Anonymous. They're trying to put the X back in Christmas.

Every Christmas is the same. Wouldn't it be wonderful if something different happened this year? Like 200 soldiers at a lonely outpost in the Aleutians, volunteering to fly down to Los Angeles to entertain Bob Hope?

You know, if you ever got what's really coming to you—you'd have a heluva Christmas!

And so we come to my favorite Christmas story—the one about the Russian named Rudolph who looked out of his Moscow window and said: "It's raining." His wife looked up from her knitting and disagreed: "It's snowing." Whereupon Rudolph went into a tantrum: "It's raining, dammit! I said it's raining—and Rudolph the Red knows rain, dear!"

IF YOU GO IN FOR HOME-MADE CHRISTMAS CARDS, THE FOLLOWING SENTIMENTS MAY BE TO YOUR LIKING: Merry Christmas! An ounce of Arpege has been sent to Zsa Zsa Gabor in your name. . . . OR: We have donated to Alcoholics Anonymous in your name: Five Drunks. . . .

My son gave me a wonderful card for Christmas. Why it must have taken him months to make it. I know, 'cause it says HAPPY FATHER'S DAY on it!

Here it is the middle of January and we're still cleaning up from Christmas. Last week we cleaned out our checking account; this week we cleaned out our savings account.

CHRISTMAS PRESENTS

Here it is Christmas again—when you buy this year's presents with next year's money.

There's all kinds of Christmas presents. One Fifth Avenue jewelry store is offering a diamond pendant and matching earrings for $140,000—gift-wrapping 50¢ extra.

One salesgirl wanted to sell me perfume—$10 an ounce! I told her: "$10 an ounce? You must be outta your mind. That's $260 a fifth!"

I always give my wife her present on December 15th. That way she can still exchange it in time for Christmas.

My wife's the subtle type. When she says she's dreaming of a white Christmas—she means ermine.

Last Christmas I gave her something worth 50 dollars—a $100 bill!

That's what I like about getting money for Christmas—it's always the right size.

Isn't it terrible how commercial Christmas is getting? Just yesterday I heard an announcer say: "Twas the night before Christmas and all through the house, not a creature was stirring— (BRIGHTLY) They had a Mixmaster!"

If you wanna give something different this Christmas—how about a Sterling Silver monkey wrench—for tightening loose dandruff?

By the way, I want to remind all you people there are only seven shopping days till Christmas. I take a size 15½ shirt; 11½ socks; I like red ties—and my hand grip fits the wheel of a Lincoln Continental.

I got such practical presents this year—like this chronometer watch. It's so informative. Gives you such helpful information as the time, barometer readings, lunar cycles, wind velocity. For instance (STUDY THE FACE INTENTLY FOR A FEW SECONDS), in exactly five seconds, it'll be low tide in Rangoon!

I had a miserable Christmas. My mother-in-law came to visit and she's such a comic. Gave us a set of matched towels marked: HERS and ITS.

My mother-in-law gave me a Christmas necktie—and I won't say how many colors it has—but it's in a clash by itself!

My mother-in-law gave me a shirt for Christmas—size 14. Which is nice, only I take a 16½. I just sent her a note: "Thanks for the present. I'd like to say more—only I'm all choked up!"

CHRISTMESS: five minutes after the gifts are opened.

CHRISTMAS TOYS

We're going through our Christmas Period now. Every night I come home and the kids are so courteous, so helpful, so quiet— I have to check the address to make sure I'm in the right house.

Remember the good old days? When kids asked for electric trains rather than a satellite station?

I'm beginning to wonder if it was a good idea giving the six-year-old one of those rockets that actually blast off. As of this morning, we've got the only cat in the neighborhood who knows what our house looks like from 300 feet up!

For Christmas I gave my kid a chemistry set and now I'm getting worried. The last time I tried to spank him, he held up a vial and yelled: "Lay one finger on me and we'll all go up together!"

It's fascinating the things you see in toy stores now. I understand they don't call them kiddie cars anymore—tot rods!

I can't get over the prices of toys. Remember the good old days, when you could go in a department store and buy a doll for a dollar? Or a *good* one for two dollars? . . . Did you ever expect to see the time when grocery chains'd have them on sale—for ten dollars? And you were glad to pay it, 'cause your daughter wanted the 30 dollar one advertised downtown? . . . But you really get your money's worth. They walk, talk, wet and fret; sigh, cry, weep and sleep. One of them is so human, every Saturday morning it asks for an allowance. . . .

I've got a Christmas toy that's gonna make me a fortune. When the kids are through playing—it puts itself away!

CIGARETTES

Have you noticed that most people who give up smoking substitute something for it? Irritability!

I love the one about the TV announcer who took a long pull on a cigarette, exhaled slowly, turned to the camera and said: "Man, that's real cancer!"

Believe me, this cancer scare has got me worried. I won't even go out with cigarette girls any more.

For years we've been reading about mice getting cancer from

cigarettes. It's a pleasure to hear that Washington is finally gonna do something about it. As of Monday, it'll be against the law to sell cigarettes to mice.

Talk about shrewd sales gimmicks—how about that new cigarette that gives you ten trading stamps with every package? And when you get 50,000 trading stamps—you get a free cancer operation.

Do you really think there are so few cigar store Indians left—'cause lung cancer got 'em all?

I know a guy who's ruined himself trying to keep healthy. Really! He just got a hernia trying to inhale one of those filtered cigarettes.

Those tobacco companies are really thinking. First they had King-Size cigarettes—then filter-tips. Now they're putting out Queen-Size cigarettes—same as the others only they have a bigger butt.

Everything's getting so complicated. Yesterday I went into a department store and ordered a carton of cigarettes. The girl said: "Plain or filtered?" I said: "Plain." She said: "King-size or regular?" I said: "Regular." She said: "Flip-top box or packaged?" I said: "Packaged." She said: "Cash or charge?" I said: "Cash." She said: "Take it or delivered?" I said: "Never mind. I've kicked the habit!"

I understand that one of the cigarette companies is planning to produce its own hoss opera. They're calling the hero Phil Terr—and he'll have the smoothest draw in the West!

You know what impresses me about those TV cowboys? The way they roll their own cigarettes. I saw one last night who was so good, the cigarettes he rolled had filter-tips!

They're always coming out with something new. Now they've got the drinking man's cigarette. Gin tobacco with a vermouth filter.

It doesn't make sense—like smoking filter-tip marijuanas.

Doctors are claiming heavy smoking causes premature births.

Now isn't that ridiculous? I know a girl who had a premature baby—two months after the wedding and she never took a puff!

COFFEE BREAKS

I wonder what they call the coffee break at the Lipton Tea Company?

It shows you what a blasé era we're living in. Yesterday I heard a guy call up a drugstore and order: "Three packs of reefers; a quarter pound of heroin; three ounces of marijuana; a cheese Danish and coffee." . . . Man, is that gonna be a coffee break! . . .

Do you realize it only took six days to create the world? Just shows you what can be done if you don't take coffee breaks!

Let's face it, we don't have to worry about Communism in this country. If a Communist yelled: "Workers arise!"—they'd all think it was time for the coffee break.

COLLEGE

June—when 2,000,000 graduates leave college to look for positions —and wind up getting jobs.

S: I happen to be a college graduate. Took nuclear physics for four years.
C: You took nuclear physics for four years?
S: That's right.
C: How did you ever survive the first one?

I know one college senior who took six years of French—and it came in very handy. Helped him make out the English titles on Brigitte Bardot pictures.

He's a college man. You've heard of the rambling wrecks from Georgia Tech? Well—he's sort of a total loss from Holy Cross.

45

I'll tell you how crowded the colleges are—I know a nine-foot-tall basketball player—and even *he* can't get in one!

What's so awful about panty raids? Everybody enjoys them—the boys, the girls, the local lingerie shop.

My son is getting out of college and not a dollar too soon! He's already finished four years and a bank account. . . . Last month he wrote me a letter: "Dear Pop—haven't heard from you in weeks. Send me a check so I'll know you're all right!" . . .

Even when he graduated from college, it was apparent this man had what it takes to be a big success—rich parents!

FACULTY: the people who get what's left, after the football coach receives his salary.

I'll never forget my senior year in college. That's when I got my letter. It was from the coach—suggesting I take up chess.

I won't say how I spent my four years at college—but they made me honorary chugalug on the highball team.

Man, did we have a team! We played Notre Dame and beat the pants offa them! We played Georgia Tech and beat the pants offa them! We played Syracuse and beat the pants offa them! Then we played Vassar. . . . Spoil-sports! . . .

It's one of those highly ethical colleges that doesn't believe in buying its football players. All it gives them is room, board, and $200 a week toward their textbooks.

I know one football player who's been in college for 13 years. It's kind of a sad story. He can run and he can kick—but he can't pass.

It's reassuring to see that colleges are putting the emphasis on education again. One school has gotten so strict, it won't even give a football player his letter, unless he can tell which one it is.

I understand one of the bigger colleges is trying a very unusual experiment this fall. It's putting students on the football team.

COMEDY STYLES

Have you noticed how the big thing in comedy now is to tell jokes while sitting on a stool? Agents are looking high and low for comics who can think on their seat.

These intellectual comics are really something. You go to a nightclub and they don't check your age any more—your IQ.

There they go, the Huntley-Brinkley of comedy.

Who writes your material? Picasso?

Isn't he wonderful? It's positively inspiring to see a comic come up here and get laughs—*without* falling into the swimming pool.

There's one good thing about doing comedy. If you don't get yocks, you get laughs—if you don't get laughs, you get chuckles— if you don't get chuckles, you get smiles—and if you don't get smiles, you get ulcers. You always wind up with something!

Now the big thing is sick comics—and some of them aren't even sick, they're stretcher cases.

We were gonna have a sick comic on the bill tonight but that's off. He called in well a few minutes ago.

This man does an act that's so sick, he could collect from Blue Cross.

I've heard of sick comics but this boy is a terminal case.

IF YOU HAVE LARYNGITIS: You've been hearing about all these sick comics? (POINT AT YOURSELF AND NOD YOUR HEAD) All the rest are fakes!

One sick comic was so successful, he could afford to go to a psychiatrist twice a day. Got cured—now he's a bum again. . . . And what makes it even worse, the doctor's doing his act! . . .

Have you bought any greeting cards lately? No matter what the occasion is—Christmas, Easter, Mother's Day—they're all sick!

Sick, sick, sick! Some of them are so sick, you need a prescription to buy them.

Remember Lum and Abner? Seems like another era. Here were two fellas who sometimes spent 15 minutes to get a chuckle. Fabulously successful. Now if you don't get a yock while bringing the microphone up to your height—you're dead!

COMMERCIALS

Some of those commercials are fantastic. I saw one this morning that starts off with a huge picture of the Venus de Milo. Followed by the announcer saying: "See what happens when you use too strong a detergent?"

Man, I'm pooped! This morning I got a headache and all day long —two aspirin and three Bufferin were chasing it around my bloodstream.

INCURABLE OPTIMIST: someone who watches that TV commercial every night—and keeps betting on the aspirin to win!

(IN A VERY AGGRESSIVE VOICE DECLARE:) They said it couldn't be done! (THEN SWISHILY:) So I didn't even try.

Do you think Lucky Strike green will ever come back from the war?

That was the Gillette Razor Song: NOBODY KNOWS THE STUBBLE I'VE SEEN.

I'll never forget the first shaving commercial I ever saw. I was so impressed, I went right out, bought the product, took one long swipe (PANTOMIME FROM THE SIDEBURN, DOWN THE CHEEK AND UNDER THE CHIN IN ONE FAST-SWEEPING MOTION) just the way they did it on TV. Bled for three weeks . . . 103 stitches and Blue Cross is still arguing about the bill. . . .

I must have watched 10,000 shaving commercials and I still have one question about them. They always show the players shaving *after* the game—like we fans don't count.

If not completely satisfied, just return the unused portion of the bottle—and we'll cheerfully refund the unused portion of your money.

(SHY AWAY FROM THE LIGHT, HOLDING UP YOUR ARMS AS PROTECTION AGAINST IT:) "I make up to $200 a week growing mushrooms in my cellar!"

Have you noticed how sneaky the cops are getting? With psychology, no less! They've got a new sign down on Broadway: FOR THAT RUN DOWN FEELING—WHY NOT TRY JAYWALKING?

Did you hear the one about the practical joker in Sing Sing who kept putting a little sign on the electric chair: "You can be sure, if it's Westinghouse!"

I just found out why there are so many commercials on that show. It gives the hero time to reload.

I just had a shattering experience. I put some of that toothpaste that tastes like bourbon—on one of those toothbrushes that taste like strawberry.

Life is getting so hectic, they're bringing out a new toothpaste with hidden, invisible food particles already in it—for people who don't have time to eat between brushings!

One toothpaste manufacturer has something that's guaranteed to remove film. Wouldn't it be wonderful if TV bought some?

Those deodorant commercials are really doing their bit for togetherness—'cause the family that sprays together, stays together!

This show is sponsored by the makers of Penicillin—the ideal gift for the person who has everything.

COOKING

Where else but in America? The scene is a supermarket. A young mother is pushing a cart down an aisle with her five-year-old scouting ten feet in advance for his favorites. Suddenly he runs up to a display, pulls out a package, and runs back to her with it. She smiles tolerantly and says: "No, Tommy, put it back. You have to cook that."

This age is turning out a special breed of girl. She can turn your head with her flattery—and your stomach with her cooking.

Men! If you want to lose weight, I've got a great new diet for you. Only eat when your wife cooks!

You can't imagine the things she gives me for dinner. If the electric can opener ever blew a fuse, I'd starve to death.

That's the trouble with girls today. All they can do is thaw foods. Why can't they open cans like their mothers did?

My wife keeps giving me those dinners that come in aluminum bags. You know the kind—you drop them in boiling water for five minutes and serve. Really—it's wonderful. Last night she boiled the most delicious steak (MUG NAUSEA). . . . Some men married cooks—I married a direction reader. . . .

Now my wife's mad at me. She gave me one of those TV dinners last night—the fifth this week—and after it was all over I said: "That was wonderful, dear. My compliments to the oven!"

I don't mind my wife giving me all those TV dinners—but when she starts heating up the leftovers and calling them re-runs—

I've been fed so many TV dinners—yesterday I broke out in a test pattern.

My wife's cooking is so bad, we've got the only mice in town getting CARE packages from across the street.

But I found a way to settle her hash. I take two Tums—she's a terrible cook!

Last week she gave me a stack of pancakes for breakfast. I think the recipe came from Decca.

And her cooking! This is the only girl who can take an hour and a quarter to make minute rice!

C: It's so embarrassing. Every morning she comes over with two cups and tries to borrow sugar.
S: What's so embarrassing about that?
C: They're C cups!

But I've got to admit her cooking's improving. Now when she makes oatmeal, all the lumps are bite-size.

Can my wife cook? She's a perfectionist! Yesterday she was in the supermarket squeezing cans of beans to make sure they were fresh!

I understand the delicatessen is having a lot of trouble with her too. She keeps sending the food back and keeping the delivery boys.

CREDIT CARDS

This credit card craze is really something. It's getting to the point where the only people you see with cash these days are toll collectors.

It's getting so bad on Madison Avenue, if you wanna pay cash, you have to show your Diner's Club card as a reference.

Did you hear about the Madison Avenue executive who lost his appeal to women? Misplaced his Diner's Club card.

CREDIT CARD: sort of a printed I O U.

Nervy? He's the type who'd take out an American Express credit card and try to pay for it through the Diner's Club.

I guess you read about that kid who got hold of some credit cards and ran up a $10,000 bill. Now they're gonna prosecute him—for impersonating a government economist.

Out in Hollywood, they're calling dexedrine tablets Credit Cards. Use enough of them and do you get a charge!

We're now members of the Currency Club. It's a new idea. You pay your bill with cash—and get your change in credit cards.

You make sense like a Diner's Club card at the Automat.

It's one of those rare strokes of good fortune—like your wife losing her credit cards on December 20th.

Cheap? He's the type who gets mad because gum machines won't take credit cards!

Remember when CHARGE! meant the Light Brigade instead of the Diner's Club?

CRIME

The New York vice cops have really been on the job. They raided a place last week and it's fascinating the way the papers described it. They said it was sort of a professional building with girls to match. . . . I mean, I've heard of co-operative apartment owners, but this is ridiculous! . . .

I don't know what this city is coming to. I hear it's getting so bad after midnight, even the muggers travel in pairs.

I've heard of crazy thieves, but do you realize they're putting up a new sign tomorrow: WATCH YOUR HAT, COAT AND OLIVE?

I hear the FBI has a new definition of counterfeiters—people who make Brand X money.

I know a guy who's in Leavenworth because he was making big money. About a third of an inch too big.

Talk about no guts—I know a counterfeiter who's chicken. Still has the first dollar he ever made.

So this crook went up to the cashier in a Chinese restaurant, pulled out a gun and said: "Gimme $200 in fives, tens, and twenties—to go!"

Did you hear about the convict who was an incurable practical joker? Kept making toast on the electric chair.

The whole trend in modern penology is to make the prisoner feel he's wanted. To convert the penitentiary into his home away from home. . . . I know one warden who's going the limit. He's having his wife make slip covers for the electric chair. . . .

CUBA

When it comes to Castro—there's only one thing that keeps him from being a bare-faced liar.

As far as I'm concerned, Castro is a four-dimensional SOB. An SOB no matter how you look at him.

There's no question that Castro is helping the Cuban people. I just read where he's brought the five-day week to all firing squads. . . . Man, when you complain of shooting pains down there—you ain't just talkin'. . . .

Remember the good old days in Cuba—when "to the wall" meant Jai-Alai?

Talk about great ideas. I know a fella who's opened an evening wear shop in Havana. Features bullet-proof cummerbunds.

Can you think of anything more dated than a Cuban travel poster?

We better watch out for Cuba, 'cause right now, it's the fastest growing country in the world. Its government is in Russia; its bankers are in Red China; its people are in Miami; and its economy is going to Hell.

D

DANCING

Now the big thing is belly dancers. Like the whole country is going to pots.

I understand he does all of the choreography for Bonanza.

You've never seen such a co-operative dancing school. Why they've even got concave instructors for very fat students.

I do a terrific watusi and I never took a lesson in my life. All I do is tie my shoelaces together and fox trot.

DEFINITIONS

ACOUSTIC: an instrument used in shooting pool.

ANTIQUE SHOP: where the merchandise is old but the prices are real modern.

ATHEIST: a teenager who doesn't believe in the Beatles.

BARON FRANKENSTEIN: the one who started all this do-it-yourself jazz.

BRIDGE PLAYER: one who learns to take it on the shin.

BRUSSEL SPROUTS: cabbages on Metrecal.

BUSINESS SLUMP: when sales are down 10% and sales meetings are up 100%.

CENTRAL AMERICA: where presidents expire before their terms do.

CHISELER: a guy who follows you into a revolving door and comes out first.

CUTICLE: a delightful itch.

EGGHEAD: a guy who's found something more interesting than women.

ELDERLY WOLF: one who's not gonna lust much longer.

FALL: when the kids stop stealing convertibles and switch to hard-tops.

GOLD TOOTH: a flash in the pan.

HIGHWAY ROBBERY: the price of new cars.

HOLLYWOOD: where they put beautiful frames in pictures.

IGNORAMUS: a guy who doesn't know the meaning of a word you learned yesterday.

MADAM: for whom the belles toil.

MATERNITY DRESS: the original space suit.

MEDIEVAL: partly no good.

MESS: the one thing every man makes in a home workshop.

MINK: a tranquilizer for women.

MISOGYNIST: if all the women in the world were laid end to end, he'd get a steamroller.

MOTHER: the one who, on Christmas Day, separates the men from the toys.

MUMMY: an Egyptian who was pressed for time.

OLD-TIMER: someone who can remember when it took a lot more onions to smother a $2.00 steak.

OLD WIVES' TALES: what brings them to Metrecal.

OPTIMIST: someone who thinks cars will cost $8,000 by 1970.
PESSIMIST: someone who thinks cars will cost 8,000 rubles by 1970.

OUT OF BOUNDS: a pooped kangaroo.

OVEREATING: what makes you thick to your stomach.

PEDESTRIAN: a fella who ignores his wife when she tells him they need two cars.

PEEPING TOM: a Doubting Thomas in search of the facts.

PHONY: someone who sends a postal card with the message: "Enclosed please find check."

PRACTICAL NURSE: one who marries a rich, elderly patient.

SCENE STEALER: the guy who erects billboards.

SILLY GAME: one your wife can beat you at.

STERN DISCIPLINE: spanking.

SUCCESS: when you have your name in everything but the telephone directory.

SUMMER REPLACEMENT: autumn.

UNCANNY: the way grandma fixed dinner.

UNDER SEPARATE COVER: twin beds.

UNTOUCHABLES: people you can't borrow money from.

VIRUS: what people who can't spell pneumonia get.

DIVORCE

I once knew a woman who had 16 children and got a divorce for compatibility.

ALIMONY: Bounty from the Mutiny.

ALIMONY: the marital version of "Fly now, pay later!"

The most awful thing about a divorce—is that somewhere, perhaps miles apart, two mothers are nodding their heads and saying: "See? I told you so!"

DOCTORS

Do you think it's in bad taste for an obstetrician to refer to some of his clientele as "accident cases?"

Did you read about that doctor who was arrested for making love to six women patients in a row? Is that what they mean by socialized medicine? . . . And talking about patience—that sixth one must have had some. . . .

It must be wonderful to be a doctor. In what other job could you ask a girl to take her clothes off, look her over at your leisure, and then send a bill to her husband?

My impression of a French doctor getting a phone call: "Allo, Zis iss who? Brigitte Bardot? You sprained your big toe? I'll get my stethoscope and be right over!"

I haven't had so much fun since I went to the (SUMMER HOTEL) and registered as an unmarried doctor.

Did you hear the one about the comic who became a famous obstetrician? They always said he had a fabulous delivery.

Then there's the MD who got a call from a very excited woman: "Doctor! Doctor! My dog just swallowed 30 Bufferins. What should I do?" So the doctor answered: "Give him a headache, what else?"

Last year, Americans spent more than eighteen billion dollars on medical care. And it's really doing the job. More and more doctors are getting well.

Did you hear the one about the nervous surgeon who was finally discharged from the hospital? It wasn't so much all the patients he lost—it was those deep gashes he made in the operating table.

What a great idea for starting off a medical association dinner—split-fee soup!

DOGS

Dog lovers of the world, unite! Write City Hall today and tell 'em we must have midget fire hydrants for Pekingese! We must!

Did you hear the one about the rich old lady who sent her pet Pomeranian to Berlitz to learn a foreign language? All her friends said: "Don't be ridiculous! How can a poor dumb animal learn a foreign language?" And the dog looked up, arched its back and said: "Meow!"

We used to have the smartest French poodle in the world. In fact, whenever we had steak, he'd come up to the table and say: "Save si bone!"

So this big energetic Boxer is put in a kennel for the summer and meets this little Poodle. "What's your name?" asks the Poodle. The Boxer shakes his head: "Ain't really sure—but I think it's Downboy!"

It doesn't make sense—like giving someone a $5,000 Persian Rug and a puppy.

He's the type who's always fighting for unpopular causes—like asking the Mayor to build sheltered fire hydrants for bashful dogs.

For Christmas she gave me a sheep dog. Mind you, it's not that I'm against sheep dogs. It's just that I'm used to a dog that has fleas. This one has moths!

Did you hear the one about the bulldog Yale got for a mascot who's so loyal, when he's overheated he Ivy League pants?

I'm not gonna board the dog at a kennel this summer. Who needs it? I'll give him a Diner's Club card. Let him get along on his own.

DRINKING

AFTER YOU FINISH A GLASS OF WATER: There! That takes care of the chasers for the evening.

I make it a practice never to drink before noon. Fortunately, it happens to be noon in Bangkok.

Take it easy, honey. One more drink and you're gonna be knocked uncautious!

It's a funny thing about men sitting at bars. They're all there for one of two reasons. Either they have no wife to go home to—or they do.

I like the guys who go into saloons, pound on the bar and say: "Gimme four fingers of bourbon—and a thumb of soda!"

Kind of an embarrassing thing happened last night. My wife had a Scotch on the Rocks as a nightcap; then went up to kiss Junior goodnight. He opens his eyes and says: "Mommy, you're wearing Daddy's perfume!"

I've been drinking so much Scotch, I don't snore any more—I burrrrr.

If you're driving home after the show and you've been living it up a little—be sure to make your last drink—a stiff one, 'cause you gotta be loaded to face the traffic out there.

When you drink like that, you're not out to have a good time. You're just committing suicide on the installment plan.

What a party! First the ice was broken—quickly followed by glasses, dishes and furniture.

It's all right to be a hypochondriac—but who makes Irish coffee with Sanka?

Have you noticed the way he's nursed that drink for the last two hours? Yes, sir! He's doing *his* bit to curb runaway inflation!

So this Madison Avenue executive goes up to Yorkville, walks into a typical German bar, they've even got a sign up saying: LAWRENCE WELK SPOKEN HERE . . . and says: "Dry martini, please." And the bartender mixes three of them. . . .

To all you horse-players in the audience I can recommend our Long Shot Martini. It's 20 to 1.

We were drinking Option Martinis. Three and they pick you up.

It's fascinating being married to a woman who doesn't drink. Last night we had the boss to dinner and as I'm putting his coat in the closet, I could hear her saying: "We didn't have any vermouth to put in the martinis—so I used marshmallow topping instead."

It's the latest thing—skimmed vermouth for fat martini drinkers.

This Russian Roulette craze is really getting around. I understand Alcoholics Anonymous has its own version. They pass six glasses of tomato juice around—and one of them is a Bloody Mary.

And for those of you who really want something different—go back to the bar and ask for Geritol with a slug of vodka in it. It's sort of a Tired Bloody Mary.

My local bar has its own Christmas motif. A bare tree, 200 ornaments at the base, and a sign saying: WHY NOT HANG ONE ON? . . . And you'd be surprised how many do! . . . Some of their unsteadiest customers, among others. . . .

You know what I hate? Those gift decanters of liquor. Confusing? Last night I drank a fifth of cologne by mistake. . . . Without my glasses it looked like Schenley No. 5. . . .

We've still got Prohibition on a local level. I know one town in Kansas that's so dry, Dean Martin records are sold under the counter.

JACQUES WURZBURGER: A fine beer is like a fine woman—it has a good head, a full body, and makes you want to come back for more.

DRIVE-IN MOVIES

I know one drive-in movie that shows American films with German sub-titles. They're out to get the Volkswagen business.

It doesn't make sense—like showing THE PERILS OF PAULINE in drive-in movies. Someone hisses the villain and eighteen people get out to look for flats.

I won't say how this picture is doing, but when it plays drive-in movies, people ask for their gas back. . . . It's the heartrending story of a suburban couple on the verge of divorce who decide to give their marriage one last try—for the sake of the parakeet. . . .

You haven't seen drive-in movies until you've seen the Texas variety. One of them has a screen so big, they show next week's movies too.

This transition from movie palaces to drive-ins has really had far-reaching consequences. Girls have gone from losing their shoes to much more important things.

Did you hear about the couple who saw CLEOPATRA at a drive-in movie—and loved every minute of it?

I haven't been so shocked since I took an advanced course in Biology—everything from the birds and bees to Drive-In Movies.

There's nothing more interesting than seeing a murder mystery in a drive-in theatre—'cause even after the movie is over, no one knows who did it!

There are three types who go to drive-in movies—those who watch the pictures; those who don't watch the pictures—and those who keep focusing their rear-view mirrors.

WANTED: Tow truck and driver as bouncer in drive-in movie.

DRIVING

Talk about excitement! I drove my little MG here tonight, turned a corner, stuck out my arm to signal, almost ruined a cop!

So this cool cop pulls the Jaguar pilot to the side of the road and says: "Daddy-o, didn't you see that red light you just buzzed through?" And the cat looks at him bug-eyed: "Red light? No, Man, I didn't even see the house!"

Those little cars have all kinds of advantages. Just this morning a motorcycle cop was chasing my Volkswagen. I knew I couldn't outrun him so I did the next best thing. Drove up on the sidewalk and got lost in a crowd!

Did you read about that little Kentucky town that's having such a big traffic controversy? The mayor wants to make Main Street one way—and there's no other street!

We were kinda lucky the last fifty miles. They had the highway open while the detour was being repaired.

Summer's almost here. People'll be out driving again. And I've got a suggestion for every Highway Commissioner in the United States. Don't put up those signs saying DRIVE SLOW—POPULATED AREA. Nobody pays any attention to them. Use psychology! Put some up reading: CAUTION! NUDIST COLONY CROSSING. . . . It'd take *me* a week to go by. . . .

Now I want you all to be careful when driving home tonight. Remember, almost 96% of all people are caused by accidents. . . . (THINK ABOUT IT.) Somehow that doesn't sound right. Accurate perhaps—but not right. . . .

They've got a very unusual way of committing suicide out in Los Angeles. You stand in a safety zone.

This parking situation is getting ridiculous. Yesterday I parked in front of the office and while I was working—a Ford came up, pushed my car ahead ten feet, took the parking spot. Then a Pontiac came up, pushed the Ford and my car up ten feet, took the parking spot. Then a Cadillac came up, pushed the Pontiac and the Ford and my car ahead ten feet, took the parking spot. You know something? My car got home 45 minutes before I did!

If you're driving home after a show, make that last drink "for the road" coffee. If you're only slightly drunk, make it a demi-tasse.

DRUNKS

I was just reading about that very unusual hospital for alcoholics they have in California. The nurses drink. The attendants drink. The doctors drink. The patients drink. They don't cure many alcoholics but my, how the time does fly!

Did you hear about that new group called the AAAAA? It's for people who are being driven to drink.

Now they've got an organization called Teetotalers Anonymous. If you feel like going on the wagon, you call this number and two drunks come over to talk to you.

You've heard of Ma Perkins? Now they've got a sequel sponsored by Alcoholics Anonymous—Ma Tini.

I won't say he's a lush—but this boy drinks like Johnny Walker needs his bottles back.

Last year someone gave him a 17 karat gold cigarette lighter. Emptied it in one gulp!

I just saw something that's absolutely unique. An electric corkscrew for the lush who has everything!

It's all right to drink, but I understand the army got the idea for flame-throwers from his breath. . . . He's the only one who blows on birthday cakes to *light* the candles. . . .

I've got a lot to be thankful for. Why at least 10 times a day for the last 15 years—I've drunk to the fact that I've never become a slave to alcohol.

TIPSY INTELLECTUAL: a fried egghead.

He's sort of an alcoholic do-it-yourself fan. All day long he wanders around the house fixing things—highballs, Old Fashioneds, Martinis.

Drink? His idea of frozen food is Scotch on the Rocks!

They say whiskey improves with age. Scotch improves with age. Bourbon improves with age. Wouldn't it be wonderful if drunks improved with age?

DRUNK: Well, if it isn't the Bourbonic Plague!

This week they're featuring something never tried before—a bourbon ice cream soda . . . for lushes with a sweet tooth. . . .

One more for the road and he's gonna need an Esso map to get to the door.

I wouldn't call him a drunk. Let's just say he's the cautious type. Figures Prohibition may come back any minute now.

Drink? This man spends $12 a week on salted peanuts alone!

How do you like that? She came in here a lush redhead—and she's going out a red-headed lush!

After the party I took her home. Gee, it was romantic. Her head was on my shoulder. Somebody else was carrying her feet.

I'll tell you how much he drank. This boy hasn't had a drink for over six months and he's still got a hangover!

Don't laugh at him. He knows what he's doing. Watch—two minutes before the check comes he'll pass out!

It's a little embarrassing. Last week he got so loaded, they made him use the freight elevator.

It's all right to drink, but at least be a little discriminating about it. I mean—you don't show up under the influence of hair tonic!

So this drunk comes home on New Year's Eve without a cent of his paycheck left. Naturally, his wife wants to know where it went. He says: "I bought something for the house." She says: "What did you buy for the house that costs $112.00?" And he says: "Eight rounds of drinks!"

E

ELECTIONS

It's Election Day in a small Russian village and all the citizens are lined up in front of City Hall. Each is handed a sealed envelope and told to drop it into the ballot box. One peasant takes the envelope and tears it open. Immediately he's surrounded by outraged officials yelling: "Comrade! Comrade! What are you doing? Don't you realize this is a secret ballot?"

Actually, there are millions of men in this country running for offices—only most of them we don't call politicans. They're known by a different name—commuters.

Personally, I'm 100% against this election—and anything else that calls for closing up bars!

Here it is election time and once again we're all gonna be amazed at how many wide open spaces there are—entirely surrounded by teeth.

It's an unfortunate thing, but at this point in every campaign—even the candidates can't stop truth decay.

What's the matter with those politicians? Why don't they give the little man what he really wants? A little woman!

And so I say to you in the interest of good municipal government, shouldn't we get rid of that DA who hasn't won a case against Perry Mason yet?

I don't do much in politics. Frankly, I've got an understanding with (CANDIDATE). I don't run for President and he doesn't do (YOUR JOB).

I understand the Democrats were gonna run a woman for President but she turned it down. Not enough closets in the White House.

Behind every new President of the United States—there stands a proud wife and a flabbergasted mother-in-law.

My wife has already informed me she doesn't want me to be President. Says she couldn't stand having all the neighbors know exactly what I make.

(CANDIDATE) says he's a candidate because he hears the call. Up till now I didn't know he was a ventriloquist.

Nobody's gonna influence my vote! I'm gonna read all the papers; hear all the speeches; examine all the literature—then draw my own confusions.

Do you ever get the feeling that the only reason we have elections is to find out if the polls were right?

Some of the politicians are being called favorite sons. As far as I'm concerned, they can finish the sentence.

What a campaign! The Democrats are calling the Republicans crooks—and the Republicans are calling the Democrats crooks. And the funny part of it is—they're both right!

I won't say one of the candidates is running scared—but you go down to his headquarters and it's nothing but a hotbed of cold feet.

——————'s making such fantastic promises, even (HIS OPPONENT)'s switching his vote.

Maybe the returns aren't all in—but you can be darn sure the candidates are.

It's only natural ——————— won the outlying districts. He was out lying in all of them.

Did you ever stop to think that (LOSING CANDIDATE) and the planet Earth have a lot in common? You see, the Earth isn't a perfect sphere. It's flattened at the poles—and so was (LOSING CANDIDATE).

Both parties campaigned for better education and in view of some of the men who were elected, you gotta admit it's needed.

NOVEMBER 5th: the day Macy's window features election-bet losers.

Personally, I'm against political jokes. Too often they get elected to office.

EMCEE LINES

Good ladies, evening and gentlemen. . . . That does it! Next time I'll rehearse *everything!* . . .

Ladies and gentlemen—I guess that takes in most of you.

Ladies and gentlemen—and those of you who are trying to be—

The show you are about to see will not be sent to our armed forces overseas—as a public service.

I like to settle down with an audience. To feel that I know them and to have them feel that they know me. It makes for a certain feeling; a silent bond; that intangible something psychologists call—rappaport.

It's kinda hard to define what a master of ceremonies is really supposed to do. In essence, he exaggerates what's coming up and makes excuses for what's gone before.

INTRODUCTION: Next, we have a young man who's done so much in so little time, it's kinda hard to exaggerate his accomplishments —but I'll do my best.

INTRODUCTION: And here she Is—the greatest thing since sliced bread— _____!

INTRODUCTION: Next, we have a little girl who was named after Joan of Arc—and not too long after her, either.

DECEMBER 26th: I'm amazed to see so many people here. I thought everybody'd be standing on the exchange line at Macy's.

Why so grim? You people are looking at me like I was your daughter's first date!

Smile! Enjoy yourselves. You people look like grammarians watching GOMER PYLE.

Is there a Mr. and Mrs. Smith in the audience? I've got a message from your baby-sitter. She wants to know where the fire extinguisher is.

SECOND SHOW OPENING: Well, good evening to all you new people in the audience and welcome once again to all you masochists staying for the second show.

CLOSING: You've been such a warm and enthusiastic audience, I want to leave you with this fond hope—may you live as long as you want to—and want to as long as you live!

CLOSING: May I say that it's usually difficult to play to a small audience—but your unwavering torpidity and warm-hearted obfuscation this evening—has more than made up for what you lack in numbers.

May you have a Christmas you'll never forget—and a New Year's you won't even remember!

And so, as Lady Godiva remarked while getting off her horse: "I come to my clothes."

F

FARMING

A farmer came into town last Saturday night and he asked how much a hamburger was. The waiter said: "$1.50." The farmer leaned over to his wife and whispered: "Bessie, do you realize we've got a cow home worth $65,000?"

I'll never forget the day I caught my hand in the milking machine. You're looking at the only man in town with a thumb 16 inches long!

There's something fresh and vital about living on a farm. Like— where else can you find people getting *up* to watch the Late, Late Show?

You can't imagine the goodwill, the scientific progress, the increase in productivity we've brought about in backward countries through technological advice and assistance. Would you believe it—as a result of our instruction, one little Asian country even practices crop rotation? Opium one year; hashish the next; back to opium. . . . These are *happy* farmers! . . .

FATHERS

As my dear old Dad used to say (SILENCE). Dad wasn't much of a talker.

I just came from a June wedding—and the father of the bride was standing off in a corner crying his eyes out—those weddings are expensive.

So these two fathers-to-be are pacing the waiting room of a maternity hospital. Suddenly, one starts grumbling: "Don't I have all the luck? This has to happen on my vacation!" And the other says: "You're complaining. This is our honeymoon!"

Tomorrow they're featuring the Father's Day Cocktail. One sip and POP!

Next week they'll be serving a Father's Day Dinner. The food'll be the same. It's just that they give the check to Mother.

This Father's Day we got together and got him something he really can use—an extension on all the bills he still owes from Mother's Day.

MIXED EMOTIONS: what you have when your kids borrow ten dollars from you to buy Father's Day presents.

You can always separate an experienced father from the novices. He's the one who if his child threatens to run away, makes the kid put it in writing.

Hollywood kids always have a problem around Father's Day. It's not so much a question of what to buy—it's who to give it to.

Did you hear the one about the expectant father who wanted to name the baby Oscar 'cause it was his best performance of the year?

I made a little contest for my family last month. I said I'd give a dollar to the one who was most obedient; who minded mother best and did everything she said. Shake hands with the winner!

All those multi-million dollar amusement parks have the same requirement. Kids under 12 must be accompanied by money and daddy.

FLORIDA

My impression of the wife of Ponce de Leon after hearing that he was leaving Spain to search for the Fountain of Youth: (HIGH, SHRILL WOMAN'S VOICE) "So, you no-good bum, you're going to Florida without me!"

I just bought some Florida real estate and I'm getting a little worried. They didn't charge me by the acre—by the gallon.

We always go to Florida in July. We figure it's the only way to avoid higher prices, higher rentals, and Hialeah.

They're always talking about that Florida orange juice. Well, you do have to admit—it *is* great with vodka. But what isn't?

You gotta admit one thing about that Florida weather—it's so wonderful, even hurricanes don't wanna leave it.

It's so hot down in Florida, women aren't even wearing their mink stoles—just the appraisals.

Last year I bought a car to go to Florida. This year I learned my lesson—I'm buying a sled!

People are heading for Florida again. For the winter—and last year they found it down there. . . . I understand if they have one more winter like last year, they're gonna take the flamingos out of Tropical Park and put in penguins. . . .

I just got back from Florida. You all know Florida—Alaska with Jai Alai games.

That Florida weather is really something. Cold? It got so bad I had to put anti-freeze in my suntan lotion.

Enough of this! Why don't we all go down to Florida and sneer at Man Tan commercials? . . . And for those of you who can't get to Florida this year—be a sport. Send a check anyway! . . .

FOOD

I hear the big food companies are working on a tearless onion— and I think they can do it. They've already given us tasteless bread.

Believe me, some day a manufacturer's gonna make a fortune putting out a breakfast cereal that'll *drain* the energy from kids!

73

(BURN A ROUND HOLE IN YOUR SHIRT AND UNDERSHIRT AT STOMACH LEVEL WHICH WILL BE CONCEALED BY YOUR SUIT JACKET. WHILE ON THE SUBJECT OF FOOD:) Man, talk about stomach acid! (THEN OPEN YOUR JACKET.) And I always thought those commercials were kidding!

Every morning I'm faced with this tremendous decision—which cereal to eat. I say to myself: "What do I want to be? A cowboy, a baseball player, or a space cadet?"

FOOTBALL

Isn't that sad about the Barber College that formed a football team? Didn't win a game all season. Seems like every time they got rolling, somebody'd get a penalty for clipping.

Did you read about that college football team in Oklahoma that finished its season with nine losses, no wins, and 380 points scored against them? I hear the coach is starting his own TV program: WHERE'S MY LINE?

I know another team with a record of 22 straight losses—yet they're happy, confident, ready for the next one! It's kinda hard to understand till you notice the olives in the water bucket. . . . They're the only team in football using a T-bagged formation. . . .

I watched the Sugar Bowl game on television. (LOSING TEAM) played like it had diabetes.

FOREIGN FILMS

Those new French pictures are awful. Why I saw one and I was actually embarrassed by it. In fact, I was even embarrassed by it the second time I saw it.

Did you read about the new hit movie that just opened in Moscow—SNOW RED AND THE SEVEN COLLECTIVISTS? . . . It's all about this beautiful, luscious, stacked mechanical engineer . . . who's sentenced to five years in Siberia for designing a sports model tractor . . . with white, sidewall lugs. . . .

It's one of those British science-fiction pictures. You can tell it's British because the Martians all carry umbrellas.

Italy has turned out its first science-fiction picture. All about these monsters from outer space who land in Rome—first they destroy the army; then they destroy the navy; then the air force. Then they make their big mistake. They pick on the Mafia!

I don't mind so much if the Russians get ahead of us in space— it's the British and the Japanese getting ahead of us in horror pictures! . . . You don't know what it does to a patriot to see the Wolfman and the Thing standing in line at the Unemployment Office. . . .

What do you think of all those International Film Festivals? They just had one in France. England won an award for the best screen play; Italy for the best casting; France for the best editing; and America for the best popcorn.

FOREIGN POLICY

There's nothing wrong with our foreign policy that faith, hope and clarity couldn't cure.

I can't understand why we're having trouble in Africa. We've got Tarzan down there—Jungle Jim, Bomba and The Phantom. Now—who's goofing?

I don't know why everybody's criticizing our foreign policy. We're still getting along with Bermuda.

GAMBLING

One woman gambled for hours, lost all her money, and in one last desperate move—put her three-year-old son on No. 16. Well, as luck would have it, she lost. But this didn't stop her. Two hours later she was home, making new chips.

It's one of those places with crooked gambling and watered liquor —where the customers will never get as loaded as the dice.

I just heard a touching story. There's a bookie down the street who changed his name to Red Cross—just so his customers' losses would be tax deductible.

Now the big thing is Indian Roulette. You sit beside a snake charmer with six big Cobras—and one of them is deaf.

Personally, I detest gambling. I'm so dead set against gambling— I'll bet 2 to 1 they'll never legalize it!

GOLF

Golfing weather's here again and I can't wait to get started. Last Fall I discovered something that's gonna take ten points off of every game. (LOOK AROUND CRAFTILY) It's called an eraser!

Isn't it amazing the way carts have taken the place of caddies on the golf course? Let's face it—they have three big advantages: They don't cost; they don't criticize; and they don't count.

If you stop to think about it, life is like that big golf tournament out in (LOCALIZE). As soon as you get out of one hole—you start heading for another.

GOVERNMENT SPENDING

I've got a brother who works for the government. Of course, if you stop to think about it, we all do.

The Senate just passed a four billion dollar foreign aid bill. That's to keep the non-committed nations in food while the Russians keep them in line.

I understand (USE APPROPRIATE TOWN OR CITY) is having financial problems. I got the answer. We secede from the Union; form a new country; then we apply to the United States for foreign aid!

Personally, I've got my own ideas on balancing the budget. We don't make any more H-bombs, see? We give one to Japan—and in three months' time, we buy all we want at half the cost.

The President's pushing for a conservative budget this year—only _____ billion dollars. _____ billion dollars! I had to bring six soda bottles back to go out tonight.

People are talking recession again but the government is moving real fast this time. It's already put 100,000 people back to work compiling unemployment statistics.

They're coming up with some great Federal projects to spend money and really turn this into a boom—like weather-stripping Alaska.

You know what I keep hoping? That somehow, someday, Washington gets the idea the Russians are spending more for (YOUR PROFESSION) than we are!

According to Washington, we're gonna have the biggest crop surplus in history and the government'll be paying out record subsidies. Personally, I think it's time something desperate and dramatic was done about the problem—like plowing under every third farmer!

This year the government has to spend $8,000,000,000 on farm subsidies—just because the farmers keep overproducing. Why it's ridiculous! Don't give 'em subsidies—give 'em defective fertilizer!

I'd like to—but I just can't throw money around on gambling, drinking and wild women. I've got a government to support.

HEALTH

I just had a crazy thought. How can a leopard tell when he's got the measles?

I don't care what you say, life is all mixed up. I'll leave it up to you. How many people in this audience went to bed last night and you weren't a bit sleepy? Then had to get up this morning when you were dead tired? This makes sense?

I won't say how popular I am, but last month I was sick for two weeks, and I only got one card saying: GET WELL SOON—and that was from Blue Cross.

I went to my doctor last week and he told me to take a hot bath before retiring—but that's ridiculous. It'll be years before I retire!

That doctor shot me so full of penicillin, every time I sneeze I cure someone.

People make such big deals of things. For instance, yesterday my doctor gave me a choice. He said it was cigarettes or cancer, one or the other. I didn't hesitate. I didn't cry about it. I gave up cancer. What's the big deal?

I've got one of those all-inclusive insurance policies. I get $500 if I'm hit by a satellite while singing HOW HIGH THE MOON?

You just can't win. I know a guy who took out $500,000 worth of life insurance policies—and he died anyway.

HI-FI

Nowadays a good conversationalist is anyone who can talk louder than the hi-fi.

It's the latest thing—silence in hi-fi—for nervous breakdowns who can afford the best!

As far as I'm concerned, hi-fi is nothing new. My dog is a woofer. The bird is a tweeter. And my mother-in-law is the loudest speaker you've ever heard!

HISTORY

Getting right down to it, you gotta admit that Andy Jackson was a real fightin' general. He didn't take nuthin' from nobody! Sort of an 1815 Frank Sinatra. . . . Why he even used pirates in his army. Can you imagine? Pirates! Nowadays the only pirates you ever see are in Pittsburgh and used car lots. . . .

You should never knock drinking. If the British in Boston had gotten stoned, stayed up all night, and charged up Bunker Hill the next morning with bloodshot eyes—things might have been very different!

For all you students of English History in the audience, have you ever heard about the spectacular new suit of armor Sir Lancelot had made up? It was such a dazzler, Sir Galahad immediately wanted to buy it. So he said: "Lance, old boy. How much?" And Lancelot replied: "For you, Galahad—buddy, five cents an ounce. After all, it's first class mail!"

HOLLYWOOD

Did you hear the one about the girl who went to Hollywood to be a movie star—but for three years she's appeared in nothing but shorts? And you just know they're never gonna show those pictures on television!

In Hollywood, everything's mixed up. If you see a mother hanging a star in her window—it has nothing to do with the army. It means she has a son who's a sheriff on TV.

Talk about children mimicking their parents, I understand Hollywood kids don't play Doctor and Nurse any more. It's Psychiatrist and Psychoneurotic!

One Hollywood producer was so impressed with the money made by The Ten Commandments—he hired a team of writers to come up with ten more.

You can tell the economy's booming again. Yes-men in Hollywood are getting so independent, they're only nodding.

It's amazing in recent years how many stars have left the movie business to go into television. Sort of like ships leaving a sinking rat.

Did you hear the one about the mermaid who wanted to be a big success in Hollywood—but she just didn't have what it takes?

SPHERES OF INFLUENCE: in Hollywood, it's bosoms.

Let's face it, there's a lot to be said for Hollywood. Where else can you go out on a blind date and wind up with your wife?

Incidentally, this happens to be the silver wedding anniversary of a very popular Hollywood star. Isn't that wonderful? The silver wedding anniversary—she's been married 25 times!

I don't wanna say how many times she's been married—but this is the only girl I know with a wash and wear bridal gown.

Liberace's having his California estate redecorated. They're painting the house and tuning the swimming pool. . . . Something had to be done. People were swimming off key. . . .

C: Hold it! Hold everything! I think I see Sophia Loren in the eighth row!
S: Sophia Loren? Are you sure?
C: Either that or it's two Yul Brynners!

Jayne Mansfield came down with a very bad chest cold. The doctor who treated her is recovering nicely.

But, as Jayne Mansfield once said to Audrey Hepburn: "You can't have everything!"

HOMES

Now the big thing is split-level homes. I can remember 20 years ago, when if you lived over a garage, you kept it to yourself.

We had a very successful housewarming last week. Invited 60 people and everybody had to bring something for the house—like a payment.

We've got a wonderful little house about ten miles out. 100 by 125 entirely surrounded by mortgages. . . . It's sort of a split-level. It wasn't always a split-level. It used to be a ranch house—then the foundation settled. . . . We've got the only house in town where you go upstairs to get to the cellar. . . .

Six rooms and 1 and ⅞ bathrooms. That fractional bathroom is really something. I can remember the salesman saying: "Most houses give you half an extra bathroom. ⅞ths is better than half, no?" I had to agree with him. So now we've got a ⅞ths bathroom —a sink, a bowl, a tub—but no pipes. . . . And the furnishings! Wall-to-wall carpeting, wall-to-wall air-conditioning; back-to-the-wall payments! . . .

We've got picture windows that bring the whole outdoors right into our living room. And on rainy days we've got kids who do the same thing.

Just got my first garden catalog of the year and it's really fascinating. Did you know they had elephant fertilizer—if you wanna grow trees with big trunks?

I even took out a subscription to a garden magazine—Weeder's Digest.

So what if the grass always looks greener on the other side of the fence? You wouldn't want their water bill.

It's crazy what a little mistake can do to you. I know a contractor who built a $3,000,000 ranch-house development and went bankrupt—just because of one silly little mistake. Put the picture windows in the bathrooms.

SHABBY ROOM: I like the decor in here—sort of early Dracula.
. . . Boy, what a good coat of fire wouldn't do for this place! . . .

I don't know what kind of lumber they used in this house, but we've got 2,000 termites dying of anemia.

I won't say it's rickety, but if you pull down the shade, the house comes with it.

This house should only be covered with paint like it is with mortgages.

HORSE RACING

That Aqueduct racetrack is really something. I understand it cost $33,000,000 to build; the grandstand is ten stories high and a fifth of a mile long; the track holds 80,000 people; has 800 mutuel windows; 16 bars; four restaurants; stables for 500 horses. All this—just to get my rent money!

The track opened today and I went out and bet $10 on the very first race. What can I tell ya? If Paul Revere would have had this horse, we'd still be under British rule!

This horse took so long to come in, the jockey carried a change of saddle.

This horse was so sway-backed the jockey had to wear roller skates.

I just heard the Kentucky Derby is a race for three-year-olds. Isn't it disgusting what some parents will do for money?

Did you ever see anything as thrilling as that Kentucky Derby? I mean—it really had me on the edge of my bar stool!

Wouldn't it be wonderful if Santa Anita was on the Diner's Club?

Two bookies were coming out of a church service. One was rapping the other on the head and saying: "How many times have I told you—it's Hallelujah, not Hialeah!"

HOTELS

I once knew a fella named John Smith. He was descended from a long line of hotel registers.

It's one of those terribly, terribly exclusive hotels. Even Room Service has an unlisted number.

Business is so bad at one hotel—chambermaids are stealing towels from the guests.

What a hotel! You've heard of the morning after? Well this place featured the night before.

This hotel has one of those tired rugs. Hasn't had a nap in years.

What a fantastic place this is! I've been here two weeks and I still don't know if I've got roller towels in my bathroom or loose wallpaper.

Incidentally, there is no truth to the rumor that Conrad Hilton is planning to buy the Leaning Tower of Pisa, convert it into a hotel, and call it The Tiltin' Hilton!

HOUSECLEANING

She's the helpful type—like the time she went out and oiled all four tires on the car 'cause they squeaked on curves.

And work! Who else scrubs the kitchen floor three times a day? I knew it'd happen. This morning she fell into the cellar. . . . Of course, her weight may have had a little to do with it. . . .

But I really shouldn't criticize her 'cause she's a wonderfully neat person. She's the type of woman who has a passion for keeping the house clean. When it rains or snows we don't have floors—wall-to-wall newspapers!

But she's really a wonderful housewife. This morning she started Fall cleaning. Threw out the Christmas Tree. . . . Not that I criticize her for not sweeping the floor. With all that junk on top of it, maybe she just can't find it. . . .

I don't know what to do with that girl. Yesterday she was cleaning out the attic and found a case of seventeen-year-old Scotch. So she threw it out. Figured it was stale.

INCOME TAX

I

INTERNAL REVENUE SERVICE: the world's most successful mail-order business.

A toast to the Internal Revenue Service! You sure gotta hand it to those boys!

I paid my income tax this morning. Now I know how a cow must feel after milking time.

There are two sayings that pretty well sum up the taxpayer's feelings: TIME IS MONEY—TIME FLIES.

It doesn't make sense—like Joe Louis becoming a tax consultant.

They just called me down to the Eternal Revenue Service. . . . I told myself: "Bob, you gotta keep a stiff upper lip!"—and friends, that's all I kept. . . . They wanted to know why I claimed 50% depreciation on *me*. Actually, it was my wife's idea. She claims I'm only half the man I used to be. . . . And they disallowed the nine dependents. Claimed parakeets *couldn't* eat *that* much! . . .

And now, a little April 15th message: Save the pennies—and the dollars will be taken care of by the Internal Revenue Service. . . . This year, the government is sending out a new simplified form. It reads: "What did you earn in 1965? Send it!" . . . But I haven't worried about income tax since the government said it could be paid by the quarter. It's wonderful. Now, every three months, I send them two bits! . . .

Did you hear the one about the housewife who didn't know whether to file a $20,000 tax return and have to explain it to her husband—or not file it and have to explain it to the government?

April is the month that tells us—not only is Washington's face on our money—but Washington's hands are on it, as well! . . . I think it's about time Washington started doing something for us taxpayers! Like printing the income tax forms on Kleenex—for people who have to pay through the nose! . . . They say that by April 15th, 40,000,000 tax returns will have been filed—not to mention all those that have been chiseled. . . . But I feel great today! Went down to the Internal Revenue Service, wrote out a check, and now I'm all paid up—to 1928. . . .

There are only two things in life we can be sure of—death and taxes. Unfortunately, they don't come in that order.

I wonder what Patrick Henry would have said about today's taxation *with* representation.

I like the one about the guy who was called down to the Internal Revenue Service to explain $80,000 in undeclared income. He shrugged his shoulders: "So my boy has a paper route. You're supposed to put *everything* down?"

What a crazy world we live in. The strong take it away from the weak; the clever take it away from the strong; and the government takes it away from everybody!

I'm a little worried about this year's income tax. I think I made it out wrong. I've got 43¢ left.

Believe me, it's getting to the point where you need more brains to make out the income tax forms than to make the income.

April 15th: the government's way of creating the rainy day we've all been saving for.

April 15th—the day when millions of Americans realize they've got an extra person on their payroll—Uncle Sam!

APRIL 15th—the time you count your blessings—just before sending them off to the Internal Revenue Service.

APRIL 15th—the day millions of Americans feel bled white and blue.

Did you read about that fella who's having a big tiff with the Internal Revenue Service? The one who says he's a split personality and he's claiming one exemption for each?

You gotta admit the government's shrewd. They've got this thing called Withholding Taxes—a sneaky way of getting at your paycheck before your wife does.

Last year I saved so much money on taxes, my wife wants us to go to Europe—I want us to go to South America—and the government wants us to go to jail.

He's the kind of an accountant you gotta admire. Last year he deducted 80 cartons of cigarettes from my income tax. Called it a loss by fire!

My idea of an optimist is a guy who sets aside two hours to do his income tax return.

I just got through paying my income tax—the government's version of Instant Poverty.

INDIANS

You look at the news—strikes, bombings, muggings—and sometimes you wonder, maybe the Indians should have had stricter immigration laws.

Did you read about that new Broadway nightclub that's run by Indians? And what a gimmick! They charge you $24 for a Manhattan!

This cancer scare is getting so bad, Indians are smoking filtered peace pipes.

Then there's the Indian hypochondriac who switched to filtered smoke signals.

I don't blame the Indians for being discouraged. They were the only ones ever to be conquered by the United States and not come out ahead.

Do you think it's true? About that American Indian couple who are sending their kids to Camp Rabinowitz for the summer?

INFLATION

I just saw a sign that says everything there is to say about inflation in just three words. It's in a little candy store—and it says: 2¢ PLAIN—5¢.

The whole country's booming. I just read of a rabbit that made his first million.

They keep saying we've licked inflation but I dunno. I was just reading that buck teeth are up to a dollar ninety-eight.

So this druggist is filling a prescription, hands his customer a little bottle with 12 pills in it, and says: "That'll be $4.50." Suddenly the phone rings and as the druggist turns to answer it, the customer puts 50¢ on the counter, walks out. The druggist turns back, spots the 50¢ and yells: "Sir! Sir! That's $4.50, not 50¢. Sir!" The guy is gone. The druggist picks up the half a buck, looks at it, shrugs, flips it into the till and mumbles: "Oh well—40¢ profit is better than nothing!"

INSULTS

AFTER CORNY JOKE: Mama, melt some butter—he's poppin' 'em tonight!

Would you mind if I called you Moses? It seems like every time you open your mouth the bull rushes.

You take good care of him, lady. Men like him don't grow on trees. They usually swing from them.

I need you like Red China needs Metrecal.

AFTER YOU TOP YOUR OPPONENT: Now—why don't you quit while you're behind?

Isn't he a gem? Believe me, after they finished him, they threw away the shovel!

This boy even looks phony. Has the type of face you'd expect to see on $3 bills.

Look at that phony! Spent the whole summer out on the beach, just so we'd think he uses Man Tan.

This man happens to be an intellectual giant—and you know how the Giants are doing.

Cheap? If he's in a pizzeria and can't finish his lasagna—he asks the waiter to put it in a take-home bag. Says he has an Italian dog.

Cheap? This boy is closer than the Dodgers' left field fence.

OBNOXIOUS HECKLER: You know what makes this even worse? He's President of my Fan Club!

Isn't she wonderful? You know, I just thought of a wonderful disguise for that girl—talent!

Nerve? He's the type who'd start a Ku Klux Klan chapter in Ghana!

We get a very high type clientele in here. Last night, someone stole the Men's Room.

There he goes—a walking tribute to the teachings of Sigmund Freud, Havelock Ellis, and Dear Abby.

Disagreeable? This boy can make enemies at Dale Carnegie classes.

Would you mind throwing your gum into neutral?

My wife wants a vacuum for Christmas. Is your head available?

I like that dress. Looks like you're suffering from tinselitis.

She's a sweet kid but there's nothing between the earrings.

Tell me, if somebody asks me what I see in you—what should I tell them?

Have you ever considered No-Cal Shampoo? It's especially made for fatheads.

This is a sick boy. Who else goes to horror pictures and roots for the monster?

Have you ever considered lacing up your mouth and renting your head as a football?

AFTER AN INSULT: Well, thank you very much for that wonderful build-down.

I won't say what kind of a paper it is—but the only ones who buy it are bird owners.

People keep calling him an expert and you all know what an expert is. Ex is sort of a has-been—and spurt is nothing but a drip under pressure!

S: Do you know who I am?
C: No, but I'm waiting to be thrilled!

You're a little confused. Just because you've got a head like a hubcap doesn't mean you're a big wheel.

BALD-HEADED MAN: He's not really mad at me. It's just that he's very upset. Spent forty minutes combing his hair and then he forgot to bring it with him.

It's just wonderful being here tonight—'cause you're my kind of group—drunks!

There's a boy with something up his sleeve—and I think it's a hanky.

Well, if it isn't Fire Island's answer to Brigitte Bardot!

WHEN A JOKE DIES: And what time would you people like to be called in the morning?

I love this place. I've come here for six consecutive years and I look back on them as the best years of my life. Which'll give you some idea what a miserable life I've been leading!

I won't say what kind of an act she does, but half her time is spent inside of banquet cakes.

His only hope in show business is for a relative to die and leave him some talent.

Isn't that sweet? He's trying to make me feel at home. And he is— 'cause I've got a miserable home.

It's such a wonderful thing having someone like him in the crowd. It's like having a parachute on a submarine.

Do you notice how calmly his date is taking all this? She figures that deep down in his wallet he's really a nice guy.

COLLEGE-AGE HECKLER: Didn't they write a song about you—The Varsity Drag?

Isn't he something? I don't mind being distracted by a Celeb— but a Celob is something else again.

I won't say how long she's been in the business, but she used to be known as the star of stage, screen and CCC Camps!

She's won numerous awards—Miss Unwed Mother of 1953.

INVENTIONS

It's the latest thing—Undo-It-Yourself Kits for Amateur Strippers!

This could be very big! Plastic song sheets for people who sing in the shower.

What a great idea! Low-cal hens for people who don't like chicken fat!

I'm working on an invention that's gonna make Christmas better than ever—guided mistletoe!

It's a brand new type of dandruff. Stops falling greasy kid stuff.

How about that furrier who crossed a mink with a gorilla and tried to breed ready-made fur coats? It would have worked too except for one thing. The sleeves were always too long.

This man is working on something that's gonna challenge the very existence of the Good Humor bar! Chocolate-covered lox on a stick!

HOLD UP A LARGE SQUARE OF RED CLOTH WITH TWO ARROWS ON IT. ONE POINTING RIGHT WITH A "YES" BESIDE IT—AND ONE POINTED LEFT WITH A "NO" BESIDE IT. "It's my latest invention—a cape for timid bull fighters!"

I won't be doing this much longer, you know. I've got an idea that's so—(LOOK AROUND, THEN SAY CONFIDENTIALLY:) I'm buying ten pounds of uranium; then I'm going up to Canada. Gonna make a fortune hunting for lost Geiger counters!

Thomas A. Edison—what a tremendous debt we owe this man! Why if he hadn't invented the incandescent lamp, tonight we'd all be watching television by candlelight!

Did you hear the one about the magician who invented his greatest trick? He tosses a huge billowing silk over a Lincoln Continental; there's a blinding flash of light; the silk is yanked away—and the Lincoln's gone! He'd make a fortune if it wasn't for one drawback—you can't examine the silk.

What a great idea! Sandpaper suspenders for people with itchy backs.

I'm currently working on a pill that's gonna revolutionize the drug industry. It's a combination tranquilizer and hormone rejuvenator. You get a tremendous desire to make love to a girl—but if you can't find one, you just don't give a darn.

JET TRAVEL

I'm gonna make one prediction and see if I'm not right. In six months, this whole jet craze'll be over! It stands to reason. If you spend $500 to go to Europe, you want it to last awhile. You don't wanna blow the whole bundle in six hours. Mark my words—the first airline that takes four days to fly to Europe, is gonna make a fortune!

Just flew in from California on a jet. Everybody was wonderful—the crew, the stewardess, the pilot. Averaged 600 miles an hour! But I was a little disappointed in the plane. Here's this brand new beautiful thing costing a million dollars—the least you could expect is to be able to open the windows.

Then there's the one about the disagreeable stewardess on the Champagne Flight: Every time you asked for something, she popped her cork.

I think jet travel is wonderful, don't you? How else can you see so much less of so much more?

The loudspeaker of the big jet clicked on and the captain's voice announced in a clear, even tone: "Now there's no cause for alarm but we felt you passengers should know that for the last three hours we've been flying without the benefit of radio-compass, radar or navigational beam—due to the breakdown of certain key components. This means that we are, in the broad sense of the word, lost—and are not quite sure in which direction we are heading. I'm sure you'll be interested to know, however—on the brighter side of the picture—that we're making excellent time!"

JOBS

I guess you heard about the executive who started to think big and got fired. Worked for a transistor firm.

The junior executive went into the President's office and said: "Sir, I just received this memo 'FROM THE DESK OF JOHN J. ROGERS'— and I'd like to speak to your desk about it."

Did you hear the one about the file clerk who went to a psychiatrist? Found herself eating alphabet soup in A to Z order.

You can't win. Last week I got into the office a half hour early every morning. Friday, the boss comes over and asks me if I'm having trouble at home.

I won't say I feel insecure, but the boss just gave me a 1966 calendar—and it only goes as far as January 15th!

I know a billing clerk who went to a psychiatrist. Kept hearing strange invoices.

If any of you people are white collar workers on a two-week vacation, my advice is get all the sun you can. 'Cause if you go back to work looking pale, the boss'll think you were out looking for another job.

We have a staggered lunch hour at the office. Everybody drinks.

It's all in the way you look at things. For instance, yesterday I passed a construction site and saw two men working. I went up to one and asked: "What are you doing?" And he answered: "I'm making $25 a day." Then I turned to the other man and asked him the same question: "What are you doing?" And he answered: "I am building a cathedral!" And would you believe it, fifteen minutes later, that man was fired—'cause he was supposed to be building a delicatessen!

He's a very distinguished author. Writes the captions for French postcards.

She's a gorgeous girl. And smart! Why just last week three different businessmen offered her a position—horizontal, as I recall it.

We were supposed to have another person here but three days ago, he was called to that great eternal resting place—got a civil service job.

Personally, I've got nothing against our police force—or, as they're sometimes referred to—the Touchables.

I don't know what to do any more. I feel just like the tailor who makes size 12 slacks. I'm always getting a little behind in my work.

Did you hear the one about the 96-pound weakling who got himself a job as a coal miner? A soft coal miner.

Personally, I think Jack the Ripper was never killed. I think he's doing my laundry this very minute.

Isn't it too bad about the neurotic laundryman who keeps losing his buttons?

I once knew a glass blower who got the hiccups. Turned out 700 crystal balls before we could stop him!

They say coffee keeps people awake. I know a guy who's kept awake by milk. He delivers it.

For those of you who are wondering how things are going in East Germany—last week a refugee escaped across the border; came to New York; was offered a job in a factory working 12 hours a day, six days a week. He said: "Who wants a part-time job?"

JULY 4th

Here it is July 4th, when we honor our country's heritage—life, liberty, and the pursuit of Green Stamps.

Let's face it, an adventurer I'm not! The only traveling I do on the 4th of July is from the TV set to the liquor cabinet—and sometimes back.

I'm afraid the time has come to bring something to your attention. The July 4th Weekend is half over—and according to the National Safety Council, so far there have been 300 less auto accidents than they predicted. Which means—you people haven't really been trying!

Things keep changing. Thirty years ago it used to be gunpowder that killed people on the 4th of July. Now it's horsepower.

JUVENILE DELINQUENCY

How times have changed. Remember 30 years ago—when a juvenile delinquent was a kid with an overdue library book?

We gotta lick this juvenile delinquency problem—figure out a way to keep kids off the streets—like building bigger poolrooms!

I just wanted to be like other ten-year-olds—play ball, go out on hikes, neck with girls, steal cars, slug cops.

Talk about crazy things, zoologists have just discovered that chickens are playing a brand new game. They stand at the side of a super highway and wait for a car to come on at 80 miles an hour. Then they dash across the road in front of the car—and the one that comes closest to getting hit, wins! Those that get scared and jump back are called Juvenile Delinquents.

Personally, I think we've gotta do something about this juvenile delinquency problem. Something desperate, like making teenagers illegal!

I understand the only people in the world who have no juvenile delinquency problem is the Eskimos—and it's all because of whale blubber. The minute a kid steps out of line, they whale him till he blubbers!

Now they've got a new slogan to curb juvenile promiscuity: Is an hour of pleasure worth a lifetime of shame? What bugs me is—how do they make it last an hour?

Personally, I'm for birth control. It's the only real cure for juvenile delinquency we've come up with.

L

LAS VEGAS

Las Vegas—those people are mad for gambling! One day I pulled into a parking space; dropped a dime in the meter; three little wheels spun around—lost my Buick!

No wonder Las Vegas is getting so crowded. No one's got the plane fare to leave!

My impression of a house detective in a Las Vegas hotel: (KNOCK ON THE MIKE HEAD). You got any money in that room?

I just got back from Las Vegas. You know what Las Vegas is— Metrecal for your wallet. . . . I had this stack of chips as tall as Gregory Peck. Two hours later—Mickey Rooney! . . . And it's quite an experience getting off the plane in Las Vegas. I dropped my bag and two seconds later I was faded! . . . But I'm just wild about it. Really! You just can't beat the sun, the climate, the people, or the slot machines. . . .

Las Vegas has the only hotels in the world, where if you call down for room service—they send up three slot machines and a changemaker.

You remember 1929—when billions went down the drain; people lost their life savings and jumped out of windows? We have the same thing nowadays only it's called a weekend in Las Vegas.

So this fella is driving across Manhattan when he hears a small, ghostly voice saying: "Go to Las Vegas! Go to Las Vegas!" On an impulse, he turns the car around and heads West. Four days later he's rolling into Las Vegas when the same voice says: "Go to the Lucky Club! Go to the Lucky Club!" So he drives to the Lucky Club, walks into the game room and the little voice is more excited now: "Go to Table Three! Go to Table Three!" And he goes to Table Three. The voice is beside itself: "Bet a thousand dollars on 26! Bet a thousand dollars on 26!" And caught up in the spirit of the thing, he whips out his wallet, pulls a thousand dollars out and throws it on number 26. The wheel spins around, the ball bounces from number to number, and finally—with a sickening clunk, drops into number 13. The fella's hysterical! "Voice!" he yells. "Voice! You tell me to come to Las Vegas, to go to the Lucky Club, to go to Table Three, to bet a thousand dollars on 26! I did everything you said and I lost. I lost a thousand dollars!" And the little voice answers: "How 'bout that! How 'bout that!"

It's such a novelty for a comedian to work a place like Las Vegas. You go in with fresh, new, expensive material—and you can do so well that the act is held over for months—by other comics.

So this Martian politician lands in Las Vegas and spends half an hour watching people play a slot machine. Finally he can stand it no longer. He goes up to it, shakes his head and says: "Son, I don't know what you're running for—but when you shake hands—smile!"

I just came back from three glorious weeks in Las Vegas where I underwent a rather unusual operation. Had my wallet removed and they didn't even give me an anesthetic.

But I did well in Las Vegas. Drove there in a $4,000 car and came back in a $20,000 bus.

I would have had a wonderful time in Las Vegas if it wasn't for the temperature. The sun was too hot and the dice were too cold.

I won't say I'm unlucky, but the last time I went to Las Vegas—I lost $42 in a gum machine.

Then I took a 9 to 5 job in Las Vegas. It wasn't a very good job but I liked the odds.

Some of those old proverbs are ridiculous. Take the one that goes: "There's safety in numbers!" You ever been to Las Vegas?

I like the one about the Martian who landed in Las Vegas, went up to one of the dealers, and said: "Take me—to the cleaners!"

Did you hear the one about the atomic scientists who went to Las Vegas for a weekend of rest and relaxation? One of them got caught up in the gambling whirl and spent all his time at the crap tables. After a while, two of his friends got a little worried. One said: "Look at poor Smythe—in there gambling like there's no tomorrow!" And the other one answered: "Maybe he *knows* something!"

You can't really call Las Vegas a city. It's more like a garbage disposal for money.

ABRAHAM LINCOLN

It's a funny thing. History tells us Lincoln once walked nine miles to borrow a book—so now they close the libraries on his birthday.

There's something about Lincoln's Birthday that does something to you inside. Why every February 12th for the last ten years—I've stopped beating my slaves!

I've had a five dollar bill in my wallet for years. I keep it for sentimental reasons—Lincoln looks like my wife.

But when it comes to honesty, Lincoln had nothing on that curio shop with the big sign out front: JUNK BOUGHT—ANTIQUES SOLD.

To paraphrase the immortal words of Abraham Lincoln—the Internal Revenue Service must love poor people; it's creating so many of them.

PRACTICAL JOKER: someone who sends Raymond Massey a birthday card on February 12th.

I like the one about the rich kid who wanted to follow in Lincoln's footsteps. So he did all his homework by the light of a roaring Shish-ke-bab.

I wonder if Carl Sandburg drives a Lincoln?

MARRIAGE

OPTIMIST: someone who goes down to City Hall to find out when his marriage license expires.

June is the month when hundreds of thousands of men take some girl to be their awful wedded wife.

I used to wonder why women did so much crying at weddings. Then I took a better look at some of the grooms.

I told her I'd make her happy if it took every dollar her father had.

There's a very unusual story behind that marriage. They met in a summer resort and they had nothing in common—but they kept fooling around until they did.

I dunno. They keep saying sex is overrated. If it is—can you imagine where everything else stands?

Some of these catered weddings are getting so extravagant it's ridiculous. I went to one where they didn't have finger bowls—everybody took a shower!

Let's face it, men, you really need a wife. Think of all the things that happen that you can't blame on the government.

Did you hear the one about the girl with the rather purple past who was finally getting married? So she went out and bought a red, white and blue nightgown with sequinned earmuffs and neon slippers for her wedding night. She figured she wanted to have *something* to surprise her husband with.

I don't want to gossip, but it was obvious *that* marriage was gonna fail. Let's face it, who sends down for a copy of TV GUIDE on your wedding night?

Did you read about that 80-year-old man who married a high school girl? At least he was realistic about it. For a wedding present he gave her a DO-IT-YOURSELF KIT.

They've got all kinds of books on marriage: HOW TO MAKE YOUR MARRIAGE WORK. Then the sequel: HOW TO MAKE YOUR HUSBAND WORK.

But she caught on quick. In less than two months she learned how to scrape toast, carrots and fenders.

My wife and I had a lot of trouble over religion. She worships money and I won't give her any.

When I was a kid, I used to hang my stockings up and find presents in them. Now I hang my pants up and find my wife in them.

My wife believes in a 50-50 type of Christmas. She signs all the cards and I sign all the checks.

I don't know how you spent the long weekend but my wife had me painting the roof, raking leaves, fixing the front steps, and cleaning out the garage. Now I know why they call it Labor Day.

Did you hear the one about the fella who took his wife to a witch doctor because she was?

Here's a silly—about two cans of paint who get married—and three months later she snuggles up to him and says: "Honey, I— I think I'm pigment!"

Western Union keeps saying: DON'T WRITE—TELEGRAPH. Well I once knew an electrician who got 30 years for wiring his wife on Valentine's Day.

I want you to know we've been married ten years and we've never had one single argument. Not one! Whenever we have a disagreement we just sit down, and reason things out in a calm, orderly manner. Last night the reasoning got so loud it took two squad cars to stop it.

A few husbands in the audience are observing their 25th wedding anniversaries—and we're gonna have two minutes of silence for them—perhaps the first they've ever heard. . . . I say observing. Their wives are celebrating it—they're observing. . . .

It's kinda funny the way things work out. I got married because I wanted a large family—and I got one—my wife's.

It's not that I mind my mother-in-law living with us—but she could have at least waited until we got married.

My wife hasn't spoken to me for three weeks. Claims I had no right to paste travel posters on the walls of her mother's bedroom.

I wanna dedicate this next number to my mother-in-law. Lovely woman. Picture Fidel Castro in toreador pants. . . . No, I really shouldn't compare her to Castro. His speeches only take four hours. . . .

I look at it this way—mother-in-laws are a lot like seeds. You don't really need them but they come with the tomato.

MARTIANS

The way things are going, I can't imagine why all these Martians wanna be taken to our leaders. They're gonna learn something?

So this spaceman climbs out of his flying saucer, goes up to a hipster standing on Times Square, and declares: "We are from Mars!" The cat looks him over and says: "Man—I dig your candy bars the most!"

Did you hear the one about the spaceship that lands on the French Riviera? A little green man jumps out, walks up to a native and says: "Take me to Brigitte Bardot! To Hell with your leader!"

Just for the record, I'd like to list the one about the Martian who landed in Central Park—and just as he was about to say: "Take me to your leader"—somebody mugged him.

So this spaceship lands on a deserted street in New York and two Martians jump out. Suddenly, one whips out his ray gun and points it at a fire hydrant. But the other one clouts him in the head and says: "You don't need a ray gun, stupid! Can't you see it's only a woman?"

And this other Martian lands in the middle of a saloon, looks around and sees a jukebox playing in the corner. Colored lights are flashing; the change mechanism is clicking; and a beautiful female voice is pouring out a song. He listens a moment, then pats the machine tenderly and says: "What's a beautiful girl like you doing in a place like this?"

Then there's the one about the neurotic Martian who landed in front of the Wurlitzer music store, looked at one of the pianos and growled: "All right, you, wipe that smile off your face!"

Two Martians land in New York and are watching Frankenstein on the Late Show. After a half hour, one nudges the other and says: "Such a lovely boy. Too bad his voice doesn't match his looks!"

The darndest things are happening. Yesterday a flying saucer landed right in the lounge. A door pops open, this little green man jumps out, walks up to the headwaiter and whispers: "Pssst, take me to your Men's Room!"

So this Martian lands smack-dab in the middle of the Steinway showroom, looks around at all the assembled pianos, and mutters to himself: "Man, do these people have dentists!"

A Martian lands in Levittown, goes up to a man watering a lawn and says: "Take me to your leader!" And he says: "I can't. She's in Monticello with the kids."

So these three Martians were walking down 42nd street, trying to find the Stork Club. Finally, one stopped the others and said: "Let's ask him for directions!"—and pointed at a fire hydrant. Whereupon the leader gave him a shot in the head and said: "Don't be ridiculous! Can't you see he's only a child?"

You gotta give waiters credit—they really know their business. Why if a Martian with eight arms, six legs, four eyes and two heads walked in, sat down, and ordered a Martini—they wouldn't serve him unless he could prove he was over eighteen.

So these Martians are standing in a clump watching the Miss Universe Contest. One by one the voluptuous contestants roll by and the space people just stare at them with their three heads and nine eyes. Finally, one of them nudges a little five-year-old Martian girl standing beside him and says: "There! See what'll happen if you don't eat your spinach!"

MEN'S CLOTHES

It's all right to be fastidious—but who puts shoe trees in sneakers?

Isn't this a lovely suit? And so reasonable. Just two installments and a change of address.

I like that tie—which shows you how much I know.

I don't wanna start a big international situation but I'm not sending my shirts to that Chinese laundry any more. You get them so nice and clean—but two hours later they're dirty again.

I like that suit. The material's so lush—like you had it cut from an old sofa.

For months now I've felt that old age was creeping up on me—but it was only cheap underwear.

EVENING CLOTHES: What do you think of this get-up? I feel like I just fell off a wedding cake.

I don't wanna cast any aspersions—but with all those cowboy boots, I'll bet Texas is the only state in the Union where more men wear high heels than women!

MIAMI

Next week I'm going to Miami for my health. That's where I left it last year.

And for all of you people going to Miami this year, let me quote an old Southern proverb that goes: "Any Yankee tourist is worth three bales of cotton—and they're a lot easier to pick!"

And to add insult to injury, they've got a motel down there named THE YANKEE CLIPPER.

You don't know what a building boom is until you've been to Miami Beach. Five more hotels and the entire state of Florida is gonna sink into the Atlantic Ocean.

Things are moving so fast, they don't even refer to "this year's hotel" any more. A place is old if the paint is dry.

Those Miami Beach hotels are really something. I was just reading that one of them hired the London Philharmonic for the season—and this is for the cocktail lounge!

And the size of those hotels! One hotel is so big, it's applying for statehood.

Those Miami hotels are so swanky. I know one where they won't even let you into the steam room without a tie and jacket.

One Miami Beach Cabaña Club is so exclusive, they had to give up swimming. Even the tide couldn't get in.

But you don't know what expensive is unless you've spent January in a Miami Beach hotel. One day I asked a bellboy for change of a dollar. He said: "Friend, around here a dollar is change!"

I hear Miami bookies have a new kind of lottery. Each day you gotta guess which'll go higher—the temperature or room rents.

The prices in those Miami Beach hotels are fantastic. I went up to one room clerk and said: "I want something quiet and restful—and it should be under $5!" So he gave me a Miltown.

I won't say it's a clip joint, but if you want to see the ocean, you drop a quarter in a slot and the Venetian blinds open for 30 minutes.

Did I stay in a clip joint down in Miami! I think it was this year's hotel at next year's prices!

I just came from Miami and the cold is getting ridiculous. I mean, it's all right to have frozen orange juice—but right off a tree?

But I'm only kidding about Miami. It's really not that cold. Why yesterday the temperature went all the way up to freezing.

Two Martians land in Miami Beach—look out the windows of their flying saucer—and see Jackie Gleason wearing a blue velvet smoking jacket, red scarf, sunglasses, and smoking a $5 cigar. One Martian nudges the other and says, "Man, this boy's *got* to be the leader!"

MIDDLE EAST

Did you hear the one about the Sultan who left a call for seven in the morning?

ARABIA: that's where everybody goes around wearing sheets. Looks like the whole country was taking a bath when the doorbell rang.

Persia! Where else can you see a girl do the Dance of the Seven Veils—with the last one covering her face?

My idea of a diplomat is that farmer who lives right on the Israeli-Jordan boundary line. The one who calls himself the Aga Kohen.

And just to add to our troubles, I just heard on the radio about a big new hurricane coming up from Israel. It's called Hurricane Becky.

Things are getting so confused out there, they ought to call it the Muddle East.

MISTAKES

WHEN YOU BOTCH SOMETHING: And so, as my future sinks slowly in the West—

I couldn't do any worse if I were Nasser doing an imitation of Hitler at a B'nai Brith dinner.

And girls, if your boy friend comes around and suggests a game of strip poker—the less shed, the better!

You help a man who's in trouble—and that man will never forget you! Never! Especially the next time he's in trouble!

What with strikes, war threats, the atom bombs, rock and roll— did you ever get the feeling we ought to go back to 1620 and start all over again?

It doesn't make sense. Like throwing away a PLAYBOY calendar, just because it's the end of the year.

A couple I know got married last month so I sent them a wedding present. This morning I got a thank-you note from the bride. She said it was just what she wanted and she'd use them every time she entertained friends. Now I'm a little worried. I gave her sheets.

And for those of you who aren't sure—the smartest time to put up the Christmas tree—is when your wife asks you to.

How wrong can you be? It's like taking Commander Whitehead for a Castro aide.

MODERN LIVING

Isn't this a wild world we're living in? At what other time in history could you find people working night and day to save up enough money to buy labor-saving devices?

We've got some real knotty economic problems to solve—like—what do we do about the tremendous concentration of wealth in the hands of air-conditioning repairmen?

They're starting to call this the Space Age—and if you've ever tried to park your car downtown, you know how ridiculous that is!

Remember when Hoover promised two cars for every garage? Well it took 30 years but we're getting close. We've got two cars for every parking space.

I had the most satisfying Labor Day weekend of my life. For three whole days I just sat in my air-conditioned living room; sipped tall drinks; and listened to traffic reports.

Next week we plan to have as our guests a panel of experts to discuss one of the most pressing problems of our time—Shall we make heavier potato chips or looser cheese dip?

How the language has changed. Remember when cat-o'-nine-tails meant a device for punishment—rather than a hipster with an active social life?

There's only one trouble with contact lenses. What do you put on in case a fight starts?

Such fascinating things in the stores! Did you see that jigsaw puzzle for people you don't like? None of the pieces quite fit together and the four corners are missing.

Talk about funny coincidences—I know a PLAYBOY photographer who uses a broad angle lens.

You businessmen oughta be ashamed of yourselves—eating in air-conditioned restaurants; working in air-conditioned offices; sleeping in air-conditioned apartments—while your families are sweating it out in (SUMMER RESORT)!

It shows you the influence of TV. They've even got teleprompters at the big intersections downtown. They tell you: "WALK"—"DON'T WALK"—I like the one that says: "RUN LIKE HELL!"

I think those WALK—DON'T WALK signs are the greatest thing to ever hit this town. It gives you something to think about while you're crossing against the light.

You gotta admit, freezers have really changed our way of life. We're not even gonna buy a turkey this Thanksgiving. We're gonna finish up last year's!

In New York a transportation company is being kidded because you can wait 15 minutes for one of their buses and then three of them will come along. Consequently, it's referred to as the Banana Line—their buses are yellow and green and they always come in bunches. This can be adapted to any large city with the same transportation problem. For instance—the Radish Line—the buses are red and they always come in bunches. The Carrot Line —the buses are orange and they always come in bunches, etc.

Remember the good old days—when students instead of teachers went after summer jobs?

Life today is made for women, not men. Let's face it, when he's born, people ask about the mother. When he's married, his wife gets all the presents. And when he dies—who goes to Florida on the insurance money?

Remember the good old days—when the still, small voice within us used to be called conscience? Instead of a transistor radio?

Do you ever read the labels on cans? You're getting such goodies as vegetable gum, U. S. certified color, sodium phosphate, benzoate of soda, and the ever-popular monosodium glutamate! . . . Makes you wanna take up fasting, doesn't it? . . .

Did you hear the one about the doctor who got a frantic call from a housewife: "Doctor! You've got to come over immediately! It's my husband! When he got up this morning, he took his vitamin pill, his ulcer pill, his tranquilizer pill, his antihistamine pill, his appetite depressant pill, and added just a little dash of benzedrine—then he lit a cigarette and there was this tremendous explosion!"

Americans are people who insist on living in the present—tense.

MONEY

The year just started and I've already saved $8,ooo. My daughter was jilted.

Well here it is April—when everybody's concerned about money. You know what money is—the stuff that things run into and people run out of.

My wife and I have the greatest gimmick in the world for saving money—a budget. Every night we work on it and by the time we get it balanced—it's too late to go anywhere.

For those of you interested in reducing your bills, it's simple. Put them on microfilm.

They say money isn't everything. That's true—but look how many things it is.

Money can't buy friends but it sure can rent them.

Is this boy making money? Yesterday he wasn't feeling so good—this morning comes a get-well card from the Internal Revenue Service.

Friend, there's an old saying: If you want to know what God thinks of money—look at the people He gives it to.

Money—you know. The stuff you use when you can't find your credit cards.

MOTHER'S DAY

Did you hear the one about the salmon who's in a terrible state of depression? Every year she lays 10,000 eggs—comes Mother's Day, not one lousy card!

You know what my idea of a sad story is? The confused little kid who was running all around a harem trying to celebrate Mother's Day.

I was gonna give Mother candy but I'm on a diet.

I don't know what this world is coming to. This morning I passed a liquor store with a big sign out front: BUY NOW FOR MOTHER'S DAY.

MOVIES

Remember the good old days—when you could spend three hours in a movie and see two pictures—instead of the first half of one?

Some of these pictures are so long, you don't know what to wear. I mean, you feel a little silly coming out into a snow storm—and you're wearing Bermuda shorts!

I took my wife to see (ANY LONG MOVIE) last night. You know, it's the longest we've been together since the honeymoon?

I understand it's one of the most expensive pictures ever made. Cost $2,000,000 just for the intermission.

Of course, Texans aren't too impressed when they spend $10,000,-000 on a picture. As one of them put it: "Son, ah spend more than that on home movies!"

After that orgy scene in CLEOPATRA, don't you feel a little silly playing Charades?

Have you seen some of the new movies they're putting out these days? I'm almost afraid to think what the Late, Late Show in 1975 is gonna be like.

Nowadays a picture's either gotta be sexy or have a sexy title to make out. For instance, they're planning to re-issue SNOW WHITE AND THE SEVEN DWARFS but they're not gonna call it that. It'll be: I WAS THE EIGHTH MAN IN HER LIFE!

I think that Walt Disney nature series is magnificent! I understand he's working on a new picture now—the epic story of a neurotic salmon—who only wants to float downstream.

Nowadays, a picture's gotta be an epic or it's nothing. Something that starts off with the end of the world—and works its way up to a climax!

One studio is spending $40,000,000 on what should be the greatest picture of all time. They're filming the first ten books of the Bible—and with the original cast!

Hollywood is doing a remake of NOAH'S ARK—and it'll be so authentic, the electricians'll use floodlights.

I just saw one of those Biblical spectacles and those scenes in the Roman Coliseum were unforgettable. Especially that scoreboard way in back: LIONS 21, CHRISTIANS 6.

I don't care what you say—Hollywood's been going downhill ever since they started making Tarzan pictures without Elmo Lincoln!

I got a wonderful idea for an adventure picture. We take Tarzan out of the wilds of darkest Africa and put him in a spot that's really dangerous—Central Park after midnight!

Now Hollywood's really got something. A psychological jungle picture! It seems Tarzan is having trouble with Jane . . . so they go to a marriage counselor . . . to find out who gets custody of Cheetah. . . .

Hollywood's making another one of those tender, homey pictures —of a young boy's transition to manhood. One scene is particularly heartwarming. He gets a razor for his 16th birthday—and he's so excited, he doesn't know what to do first—shave or slash tires.

It's kind of a sad story—about a juvenile delinquent who robs five banks—just so he'll feel wanted.

I was watching one of those ancient gangster pictures on TV last night. I'm not sure how old it was, but the getaway car was a Reo.

I was watching a movie last night that was so old—it shouldn't have even been up that late!

It's the searing, dramatic story of an innocent little country girl who was ruined in Bayonne, New Jersey—then ruined again in Hollywood, Malibu, and Miami Beach. . . . In all fairness, she doesn't really know what she's doing. It all happens while she's under the influence of money. . . .

Talk about show business miracles, I just saw this movie that was shot thirty years ago—and it only died on television last night.

There's this new movie downtown and it's really a tear-jerker. All about a poverty-stricken Russian peasant woman who's so poor she has to take in brains to wash. . . . I guess they weren't too sure of the story's pulling power 'cause they cast Jayne Mansfield as the peasant woman. . . . It's the first time I ever saw a stacked shawl! . . .

Hollywood is doing a remake of GONE WITH THE WIND and it's really gonna be something! Brigitte Bardot is playing Scarlett O'Hara. . . . Elvis Presley is gonna be Rhett Butler . . . 'cause he's so good at revolutionary movements. . . . And John Wayne is playing a dual role—General Sherman and the entire Union Army! . . . It'll be filmed in Switzerland because of a favorable tax situation . . . and other than seeing the slaves picking edelweiss instead of cotton—you'll never know the difference. . . .

Isn't it incredible how many Civil War pictures are made each year in which the Southerners are the good guys and the Northerners the bad guys? Really, I saw one last night and the Southerners were so brave, so good, so gallant—it had the only logical ending. The Confederacy won!

I got this great idea for a screenplay, see? All about a midget who wants to marry a six-foot-two-inch show girl. And we called it— GREAT EXPECTATIONS! . . . Then some guy named Dickens phones his lawyer. . . . So we called it WITHERING HEIGHTS. . . .

I once made a movie. I won't say how bad it was, but six states use it in place of capital punishment.

This picture was so bad, they had to give away dishes in the cutting room.

If you're a motion-picture theatre owner, the sweet smell of success comes from popcorn.

It's a brand new concept in moviemaking. An adult, sophisticated horror picture. I think the monster gets the girl!

One of the studios is working on a combination horror picture, musical, and Western. And what a title: THE PHANTOM OF THE HORSE OPERA.

Hollywood is turning out its first realistic science fiction picture. It's all about a spaceship that's halfway to Mars when the hero is faced with a question that almost paralyzes him with anxiety: Did he—or did he not tell the milkman to stop deliveries?

Murder mysteries are getting so sophisticated! I saw one last night that was so unusual, the butler didn't do it. In fact, no one in the picture did it. The murderer was from the Selected Short Subjects.

What a picture! This is the greatest thing in movies since dark balconies.

You think you got problems. What about 20th Century-Fox? What are they gonna call it forty years from now?

It's a new idea in movie houses. The screen's so big, they're gonna show double features simultaneously!

The movie business is really hurting. I called one theatre up and asked: "What time does the feature go on?" The manager said: "What time would you like it to go on?"

I just can't get enthused about American pictures. They all fall into the same groove. In the first four reels, he's ready but she isn't. In the next four reels, she's ready but he isn't. Then they get to the ninth reel when they're both ready but the censor isn't—so they end the picture.

MOVIE STARS

I go for the opposite sex—like Brigitte Bardot. Man, she's just about as opposite as you can get!

I understand Brigitte Bardot came down with a chest cold this week. Man, those germs really know how to live!

I hear Brigitte Bardot is gonna do a series of one-nighters in France—the opposite of anything she's ever done in the past. She'll wear a turtleneck sweater, slacks and wool stockings—and the audience'll be naked.

It probably never happened, but there's a story going around that Brigitte Bardot sidled up to a young fella at a cocktail party and said: "Tell me. If I were a genie and could grant you three wishes—what would the last two be?"

Last night I dreamt about Brigitte Bardot and it was such an intimate thing—seeing her there without any——English titles.

They were gonna make a record called BRIGITTE BARDOT SWINGS . . . but they had to call it off for technical reasons. 33 1/3 was too small—and 45 was too big. . . .

I'm just glad Jayne Mansfield is a woman. Can you imagine wasting all that on a man?

FLASH! Jayne Mansfield chosen to play the role of Juliet in new screen version of Shakespeare's classic. Producer says: "She's beautiful! She's talented! And can she lean over a balcony!"

There's only one trouble with seeing all those wonderful pictures starring Jayne Mansfield, Brigitte Bardot, Anita Ekberg, Sophia Loren—you come out and everyone looks so flat!

Remember the good old days—and silent pictures? When the only stars with big chests were men?

Wouldn't it be awful if, one day, Yul Brynner decided to grow it back—and he no longer had the choice?

Next week we're staging our annual Sonny Tufts Film Festival. Come one, come all!

And now, a special message from (CHILD STAR): (SING IN A HIGH CHILDISH VOICE) My beer is Rheingold the dry beer.

I know one star who's made a fortune—just by going out with a producer. Every time he makes a move—she makes a movie.

Did you read about that Italian movie star who measures 45-28-36? They'd show her pictures here if it wasn't for one thing. No room for the English titles!

It's no wonder Sophia Loren is getting all those terrific parts. Look at all those terrific parts she had to start with.

Sophia Loren is one girl men look up to—very, very slowly.

Personally, I think this (FOREIGN ACTRESS) is terribly overrated. I've seen six of her pictures now and I can't understand a word she's saying.

MUSIC

Presenting our first musical score of the evening—Brahms 6, Beethoven 2 at the top of the fifth.

Believe me, it's nothing to play an accordion. Anyone who can fold a road map can play an accordion.

Tonight we're giving away an autographed, hi-fidelity, binaural recording of Van Cliburn playing NOLA.

Is it true they call him the Van Gogh of the trumpet players—
'cause he just doesn't have an ear?

This fella's been playing the piano for six years—on and off. I say
on and off 'cause he's got a very slippery stool.

Music is such a wonderful thing. Just think, if there were no
music in the world—a lot of people could be put in jail for what
they do on dance floors!

C: Talk about novelty acts—I know a guy who plays THE FLIGHT
OF THE BUMBLEBEE on a string instrument.
S: What's so great about that?
C: A yo-yo?

WANTED: Zither salesman. Must not lisp.

MUSICIANS

Did you hear the one about the two musicians in India who were
watching a native magician play on a flute while a cobra swayed
in front of him? One murmured: "Talk about frantic arrangements!" and the other answered: "Who cares from arrangements?
Dig that crazy music stand!"

These two musicians are walking along, smoking iced tea—it's the
summertime . . . when an Air Force fighter, 40,000 feet up, breaks
the sound barrier. They both look up at this little dot in the sky
—and one says: "Man, I've heard of acoustics—but this is ridiculous!". . .

IF YOU'RE NEAR A DRUMMER, TILT UP THE EDGE OF ONE OF HIS CYM-
BALS, PEER UNDER IT AND YELL: "WHAT? Pot roast again?"

MUSICIAN WEARING A BEARD: Have you noticed the cat behind
the drums? With the beard? The Smith Brother with the beat?
. . . I won't say how thick it is, but for two years he's had to kiss
his wife through a straw. . . . You'd think with all the traveling
he does, he'd read a few Burma-Shave signs. . . .

NEW YEAR'S EVE

NEW YEAR'S EVE: when the old year and most of your guests pass out.

I'm gonna spend a quiet New Year's Eve—doing something constructive—like picking the names out of hotel towels.

MOST LEADING WHISKEYS AND SCOTCHES COME IN ONE GALLON BOTTLES AS WELL AS THE REGULAR FIFTHS. YOUR LOCAL LIQUOR STORE CAN ORDER ONE FOR YOU. "Personally, I'm not gonna overdo it this year. My wife and I are limiting ourselves to one bottle." HOLD UP THE GIANT-SIZED BOTTLE.

You may be interested to hear there will be no increase for New Year's Eve. The club's regular exorbitant prices will prevail!

What a New Year's Eve party! At midnight, balloons came floating down from the ceiling—the orchestra played Auld Lang Syne —champagne corks popped! I'm telling you, there wasn't a dry throat in the house!

NEW YEAR'S EVE DRUNKS: You're probably wondering why we asked them to come tonight. We figured they're so appropriate. She's 19 and he's 67.

C: I don't remember too much about New Year's Eve but we did get a ticket for riding three in the front seat.
S: What's wrong with riding three in the front seat?
C: On a motorcycle?

The Police have asked for our help in their drive against excessive New Year's drinking. So on December 31st, they're planning to draw a thin white line down the center of the dance floor—and anyone who trips over it—no more booze!

Please be careful when driving home tonight. Remember, operating a car on New Year's Eve is like playing Russian Roulette. You never know which driver is loaded.

Friends, I've only got one thing to say as this tired old year comes to a close: We've gotten through one thousand nine hundred and sixty-six of them—I'm sure we're gonna be able to get through one more.

Have you noticed how quiet New Year's Day always is? That's because 50,000,000 wives aren't speaking to 50,000,000 husbands!

Well here it is seven in the morning, New Year's Day—liquor-mortis has set in . . . and the only sound you can hear is the gentle bubbling of Bromo-Seltzer, Alka-Seltzer, and "Never again! Never again!" . . .

NEW YORK

I'll have you know I'm staying at a very exclusive location in New York—27369268 11th Avenue. It's a box car.

New York is really cracking down on traffic violators. One guy with a Volkswagen collected 78 parking tickets and they finally caught up with him. And I mean they lowered the boom. Not only did they arrest him—but they deported the car!

The traffic situation in New York is just impossible. I was telling one cop this morning: "You're giving me a ticket for parking? You should give me a medal!"

I just love Greenwich Village. Where else can you find signs reading: FIGHT MENTAL HEALTH!

It's one of those small, off-beat clubs in Greenwich Village. You know how most places have two washrooms? This one has three —HIS—HERS—and LET YOUR CONSCIENCE BE YOUR GUIDE.

And finally, let's close with the Martian who landed in Greenwich Village, walked into one of the clubs and lispthed: "Take me!"

NIGHTCLUB BUSINESS

I won't say that business has been bad this week—but I've looked at more empty seats than a tailor.

I think the boss gave up customers for Lent.

I'll tell you how bad business has been. Last night I saw the owner stealing from the bartender.

I'm not saying business is bad, but you shoulda been here last night. Somebody shoulda been here.

Business is so bad, I hear the doorman was arrested for loitering.

My impression of the boss watching a Saturday night crowd come in. (PUT ON A PAIR OF BLACK SUNGLASSES WITH A BIG WHITE DOLLAR SIGN ON EACH LENS.)

Next week we're gonna have another all-star show featuring the boss's wife at her hi-fidelity cash register.

The boss has a very simple philosophy. He figures you can't take it with you so you might as well leave it here.

The boss used to be a used-car salesman. Really. This is the only place in town where you can trade in your olive on a second Martini!

I think the funniest line in the place is that sign: OCCUPANCY BY MORE THAN 250 PEOPLE IS DANGEROUS AND UNLAWFUL , and I might add, UNLIKELY. . . .

Man, look at the crowd in here! Looks like a drive-in movie at high noon.

My agent said he was booking me into a very exclusive club—and he was right. Look at how few people they've let in!

You don't realize what an exclusive club this is. The owner won't let you stay if you're not wearing a white shirt and tie. If you don't believe me, last night he asked two ministers to leave!

NIGHTCLUBS

This happens to be the only nightclub in town with a gardener. Every morning he waters the plants, flowers, and liquor.

I won't say the whiskey is watered—but everybody calls the bartender Circumstances—'cause he alters cases.

Let's not call him a bouncer. Let's just say he operates an escort service.

It's one of those wild type clubs—where as you come in the door, they frisk you to see if you've got a gun. And if you don't—they give you one!

SMOKY CLUB: What is this—a nuclear submarine? They haven't had a window open in here in months!

I understand table nine has been waiting three hours for a round of Martinis. Don't blame the bartender. It's that sloe gin he's using.

Personally, I'm a little worried about the cashier. Been here 16 years—never asked for a raise. . . . The owner may have one more silent partner than he knows about. . . .

Some people want a loaf of bread, a jug of wine, and thou. Here we put it a different way—a bagel, booze and youze.

I don't want to quell your enthusiasm—but there's a bowling alley next door and the owner's been getting complaints from *them* about the noise in *here*.

I won't say how crowded it gets Saturday nights—but next week we're taking out the chairs and putting in subway straps.

I won't say how long I've been working nightclubs, but one day

I went outside, took a deep breath—and I heard one lung say to the other: "See? That's the stuff I've been telling you about."

Isn't this a wonderful place? Why I've seen people come in here and get the charge of their life. When they get the check, that is.

It's bad enough in here, but you go in the washroom and the walls are full of cracks—some of them not very nice!

Next week is the start of the hunting season and so on Saturday night, we're having our Annual Wild Game Night. If you know any, come on out.

Talk about switches—last night a girl was sitting at ringside with a neckline so low, she spilled herself all over a drink.

I want you to know that all the Scotch you buy in here has aged at least eight years—and it's guaranteed to do the same for you.

NUDISM

Try to convince a nudist that Ringling has the greatest show on earth.

Did you see the nudist picture that got rave reviews? One critic gave it four stares!

I understand they were gonna show a nudist picture on television—but too many people got upset. So they did the next best thing—showed it on radio.

I just saw (LATEST NUDIST FILM) and it's really a fascinating picture. You see this whole group of girls running around in tight-fitting outfits—skin!

Did you read where nudist camps are on the increase? You know what a nudist camp is—it's like, do-it-yourself burlesque.

It's so ridiculous—like a nudist wearing a muffler.

I once knew a girl nudist who never went out in the sun. I think she wanted to get married in white or some such nonsense.

O

ORCHESTRA

Man, that orchestra swings like Jayne Mansfield in a hurry!

Those boys have music in their blood. In fact, they're gonna bleed us a pint of STARDUST right now.

FLASH: Lawrence Welk has unequivocally stated that he will not play the Newport Jazz Festival this year.

That reminds me of that old German saying (RATTLE OFF A FEW SENTENCES OF MOCK GERMAN. THEN TURN TO THE ORCHESTRA AND SAY): Don't worry, fellas. It's nothing against the union.

Next week, the entire music business is joining together to pay homage to Jesse James—the only band leader who ever made it with a bank!

ORCHESTRA INSULTS

Man, something's gotta be done about this band. I don't mind a piano player who plays by ear, but this one's hard of hearing!

They're such a wonderful group—five boys with hearts of gold; wills of iron; and cars of tin.

Aren't they an interesting group? I've always had the feeling they could play for two hours—and still stump the panel on WHAT'S MY LINE?

Aren't they a wonderful bunch? They've got a style that just grows on you. Sorta like a musical fungus.

They say that by the year 2000, people will be working one day a week and resting six—a schedule the band adopted months ago.

Personally, I think the band's improved tremendously. You can tell when they're tuning up now.

That was the Bugle Call Drag—I'm sorry—Rag. There I go editorializing again.

Aren't they a wonderful group? Only three musicians but through ingenious scoring, masterful instrumentation, unbelievable orchestrations, and virtuosity bordering on genius—they give you the impression they're actually a trio.

I don't want to accuse the band of being a pack of wolves, but they just came back from a three-week engagement in the Virgin Islands—and I hear the natives are changing the name of the place.

You fellas are supposed to cut this show—not stab it to death.

S: Why don't you stop spending all of your time with morons?
C: I'd miss the band.

And now, while the boys in the band go out for their marijuana break—

How about a great big hand for the boys in the band? Let's face it—they tried. . . . I mean, if you don't have it—you don't have it. You can't fight these things. . . .

ORIENT

I'm not sure I understand this Peace Corps idea completely—but as I picture it, we go to underdeveloped countries and mingle. . . . Sort of international social directors. . . . Everybody into the school! . . .

And to the winner of this fabulous contest goes—the Taj Mahal! . . . In case of a tie, duplicate prizes will be awarded. . . .

I tell you, it's going too far! Bagels made in Japan!

I dunno. I just saw this big sign: BUY AMERICAN!—and in the lower right-hand corner there's this little rubber stamp: Made In Japan.

P

PARENTS

C: Talk about large families—my mother had 18 children and we all put her on a pedestal!
S: That's wonderful!
C: No, necessary. We had to do something to keep her away from Pop.

Then came that fateful day when Mother let the maid go—'cause Father wouldn't.

Did you hear the one about the ancient Roman parents who were very strict with their children? The kids had to be back from every orgy before eleven.

Then there's the energetic mother who arranged a match for her daughter. Now she spends most of her time refereeing it.

I'll say this—my wife is really raising our kids by the book—and I think it's PEYTON PLACE.

Summertime—when parents pack off their troubles to an old Indian Camp and smile, smile, smile!

So these parents are worried sick about their little boy—eight years old and he hasn't spoken a word. One day he looks up at breakfast and says: "Could I have a little more sugar in my oatmeal?" The parents are dumbfounded. Hysterically they cry: "You spoke! You said something! Tell us, why have you waited all these years?" The little kid shrugs his shoulders: "Up till this, everything's been okay."

I was just reading that wonderful new book on child psychology—the one with the revolutionary new approach—it sticks up for the parents. . . . And it's got an answer for everything. For instance, it's breakfast and you're saying: "Now Johnny, finish your cereal." And the kid folds his arms and says: "Motivate me!"

133

. . . The book just recommends you lean over, smiling gently all the while, and belt him in the chops! . . .

DUKE OF WINDSOR: The thing that impresses me most about America is the way parents obey their children.

PARKING LOTS

I mean it was so quiet in this club, all you could hear was the parking lot attendant creasing fenders.

Buddy, would you go outside and check with the car parker? I just got a note that your bicycle's blocking the driveway.

And how about a great big hand for the parking lot attendant—who's really been doing a bang-up job out there. . . . I understand a lot more compacts are leaving this place than ever came in. . . .

Did you read about that East German who escaped by driving a truck through a concrete wall at 60 miles an hour? They're gonna have him here next weekend—parking cars.

PERFORMING

IF YOU'RE WORKING A THEATRE WITH A PIT ORCHESTRA: This is a band? Looks more like an open grave!

SUPPER CLUB OPENING: Good evening, ladies and gentlemen—gourmets and gourmands—gluttons. . . . Welcome to the House of Heartburn! . . .

(IF YOU'RE WORKING A CLUB WITH A LARGE LINE OR A SMALL LINE ON A SMALLER FLOOR; WATCH THEM FINISH A DANCE ROUTINE, THEN COMMENT:) Girls, that was fascinating! Looked like a co-ordinated rush hour.

AFTER A BAND NUMBER: That was wonderful, fellas. Just wonderful! After the show you may each take a blonde out of petty cash!

TO PATRONS COMING IN DURING THE SHOW: Well, good evening! We almost marked you absent.

Who can understand show business? Look at me. I've got the very same chest measurement as Jayne Mansfield. Hasn't helped me a bit!

FAT STOOGE OR PARTNER: You've heard of Elvis the Pelvis? This is Kelly—

TO PARTNER: Please! Don't stare at the audience like that. Someone out there might be eating.

Have you noticed how all the big personalities are playing grandstand shows and ball parks and state fairs? Why it's opening up whole new vistas of unemployment for me.

I'll bet you people have seen dozens of comics who start off with: "A funny thing happened to me while coming out to the microphone!" Well, I don't want to seem trite or old hat—but a funny thing *did* happen to me while coming out to the microphone. I forgot my act!

IF THE AIR-CONDITIONING IS ON TOO HIGH: You've got the air-conditioner on Siberia again! . . . I don't mind cold audiences but *I* wanna be the cause! . . . Talk about unusual atmosphere—how 'bout this? Sort of a meat locker with waiters! . . .

NO LAUGHS: I know I had an act when I came in.

NO LAUGHS: I think I'm doing my Christmas flopping early this year.

Then I played Reno to break in some new material—and six weeks later I divorced my writer.

Personally, I just won't work a cheap location. Take tonight. I happen to be getting three bills for this job. Two fives and a ten.

NOISY HECKLER: I do an unusual type of act, Buddy. You have to hear me.

I'm not like some of those other comics who try to keep you all charged up. No sir! I just do a quiet, tranquil, run of the Miltown, type act.

Just got back from Hollywood where I made a Western. Played the part of a Carson City badman. I know some people think it's a little strange—a nightclub comic playing a Western villain—but it isn't, really. My big scene comes at the end where I die miserably in a half-empty saloon—and I've had ten years' experience doing just that.

I figured, why shouldn't I go into show business? The hours are good, the company's pleasant, and there's no heavy lifting. You can't beat a combination like that.

C: Everytime I hear that expression: "Something old, something new, something borrowed, and something blue"—tears come to my eyes.
S: It reminds you of your wedding?
C: No, my old act. It had a little bit of everything.

You're such a relaxed, Miltown type audience. Really, if smiles could be heard, the noise in here would be deafening!

IF SOMEONE IN A LATER ACT USES ONE OF YOUR RUNNING GAGS OR A TAG LINE USED AS A REPETITION ITEM IN YOUR ACT, COME OUT A FEW SECONDS LATER DRESSED IN A BATHROBE, SLIPPERS, PLASTIC SHOWER CAP, CARRYING A TOWEL—AND SAY: "I heard that!"

Remember, next week we're gonna have an entirely new show. We've got the wine. We've got the loaf of bread. Thou is the only thing you've gotta supply.

Really, I've never played in a nicer club, for a finer manager, in front of a more appreciative audience. (PAUSE) This is a recorded announcement.

IF YOU CLOSE THE SHOW: I'm glad they finally decided to put me on. I've been standing out there for the last 45 minutes—with my suit and material slowly going out of style.

PERSONALITY

He's the type who gives you a hydromatic handshake—no clutch.

I wouldn't go so far as to say he steals ideas. Let's just put it this way—he has a highly creative memory.

I won't say he's lazy. Let's just say he's like a blister. Doesn't show up until the work is all done.

I don't care what you say about baldness, you gotta admit it's neat.

Nervy? He's the type who'd order Yankee Pot Roast in a Selma restaurant. . . . Of course, down there they don't call it Yankee Pot Roast—Damyankee Pot Roast! . . .

I wouldn't say he's dirty—just anti-laundry.

You know what I like about you? You're an optimist! You're the type who'll bring a fifth to a New Year's Eve party and save the cork.

He's the subtle type—like a sailor on a weekend pass.

Men, it's ridiculous to waste your time wishing you were a better man. I mean, your wife's probably wishing the same thing. Duplication of effort!

It's kind of an interesting story how he became a wolf. People kept telling him he had such nice hands—they really should be on a girl.

I've heard of people who are afraid of height—but this boy gets dizzy on a thick carpet!

C: I got news for you, Buddy. There's only one thing that keeps me from belting you.
S: And what's that?
C: Fear!

He's the type who likes to delve into the great problems of life—like—why *doesn't* Bill Bailey come home?

I won't say he's eccentric, but for years he's been saving all his money to buy a new pair of ears. Claims there's holes in the ones he's got.

If you can keep your head while all about you are losing theirs, you'll be the tallest one in the crowd.

I don't have to take this, you know. I may look stupid but that doesn't mean I'm not!

People say I'm conceited but that's ridiculous. It's just that I have a fondness for the good things in life and I happen to be one of them.

Conceited? This boy and his mirror have been on a honeymoon for years.

What do you think of these teeth? Aren't they 32 of the most gorgeous things you've ever seen? Actually, only 30 are teeth. The two in the back are Chiclets.

I won't say he's cheap—but when he pays his own check, he's treating.

He's not cheap. He believes in giving till it hurts. Of course, he's very sensitive to pain.

I wouldn't say he's cheap. Let's just put it this way—he's fanatically economical. . . . I can still remember the time I borrowed a vise from him—and there was toothpaste on it. . . .

Did you hear the one about the penny-pinching girl who bought herself a one gallon economy-size can of spray deodorant? Pressed the button and blew her arm off.

He's the kind who gets caught in his own mouthtrap.

PETS

I just heard a sad story. It's about this turtle who falls in love with a German helmet.

I'm working on something that's gonna revolutionize the pet business—a goldfish that sings!

You think you've got troubles. I'll bet I'm the only one in town with a sarcastic parakeet! Yesterday I went up to the cage and said: "Can you talk? Can you talk?" And he looks at me with a sneer and says: "Yes, I can talk. Can you fly?"

PHONOGRAPH RECORDS

I feel so exotic tonight! I feel like doing something—spicy! Like going down to the record store and staring at album covers!

A disc jockey is someone who refers to Australia as being on the flip side of the earth.

It's such a lousy thing to do—like putting Lawrence Welk on unbreakable records.

I guess you read about that jazz club that had a fire—but no one got hurt because they emptied the place in 15 seconds. Someone put on a Guy Lombardo record.

C: Did you see that story in last night's paper? DISC JOCKEY WANTS GIRL WHO MEASURES 78-33 1/3-45?
S: Those are records.
C: I dare say they are!

I know a team who're just desolate because they don't have a hit record. They feel they're the only quartet in show business without a hit record. And I keep telling them: "What do you need a hit record for? You're acrobats!"

It's a wonderful new idea—a 12 inch long-playing record with an 11½ inch hole in the middle for people who don't like music.

I just came across an interesting statistic. There are only 400,000 jukeboxes in this country. I guess it just sounds like more.

POST OFFICE

The Post Office is planning to deliver its mail by missile. Isn't that fantastic—how they can get those big things through those little mail slots?

The Postmaster wants to raise the price of stamps again—but this time nobody's gonna complain. They're putting bourbon in the glue.

You'll all be interested to know that starting next week, this entire show will be sent to our Armed Forces overseas—by Parcel Post, I think.

We take so much for granted—like paper. If it wasn't for paper—if we still wrote on stone slabs—who could afford to send an airmail letter to Chicago? . . . Not that I'm knocking stone slabs, mind you. Ten of them changed my backyard into a patio! . . .

You take one look at those lines at the Post Office—and you can understand why Santa Claus delivers his presents in person.

You gotta say one thing about those Post Office people—they're honest. I sent a Christmas card to Hawaii. Put one stamp too many on it. They did the only fair thing under the circumstances. Delivered it to China. . . . Somewhere along the Yangtze River, there's a Chinaman standing in a rice paddy wondering: "Who's Orben? . . . What's a Cool Yule? . . ." Someday history books might attribute World War III to this incident! . . . Say, isn't that a wonderful title for a soft-shoe number? (SING IN STOP TIME) Way down upon the Yangtze Rivuh! . . .

Have you noticed those new signs they have up in Post Offices?

REPORT OBSCENE MAIL TO YOUR POSTMASTER! Gee, it's like some guys just can't get enough.

POVERTY

Did you hear the one about the two sparrows who were economizing? They didn't fly South for the winter—they took the bus.

I like the one about the guy who takes a taxi to bankruptcy court —then invites the driver in as a creditor.

You'll have to excuse me but I'm going through a very difficult time in a man's life. I'm too tired to work and too broke to quit.

There's a lot of things you can't bank on nowadays. My salary for one.

You gotta say this about being poor—it's inexpensive!

PRIZE FIGHTS

I'd have been a great fighter if it wasn't for one thing—a severe jaundice condition of the stomach I suffer from. Jaundice condition of the stomach—I'm a yellow belly!

Watching that fight you realize that baseball pitchers aren't the only ones who come up with no-hitters.

What a reach this guy had. Before the fight started we touched gloves and he never even left his corner.

I saw the big fight at a drive-in but it was kinda confusing. Half the time I found myself watching the wrong clinches.

More and more, the way to stay out of fights is to be the world's heavyweight champion.

PROGRESSIVE EDUCATION

Did you hear about the strict progressive school that put a sign in every room: NO SMOKING IN CLASS!—THAT IS, UNLESS YOU WANT TO.

I'm not saying what our school tax rate is—but this year, I'm listing four dependents on my income tax return—my wife, two kids, and P. S. 73.

You go to PTA meetings and suggest the little darlings may not need alcohol rubs after badminton practice—and they look at you like you're an ax murderer.

The way I see it—America's gonna be in for a big educational experience. Either we're gonna learn higher mathematics, space science, brinkmanship, and self-defense—or Russian.

It's one of those progressive nurseries. I didn't realize how progressive until last week. Two of the kids got married.

Isn't this a great educational system we're developing? Where else can you find algebra taught in third grade and spelling in college?

PSYCHIATRY

So this fella is going to a psychiatrist for six months—suddenly the headshrinker points at him and says: "You've got to give up smoking! You've got to give up smoking!" The guy is startled: "Give up smoking? That'll help me?" The doctor says: "No—but you'll stop burning holes in my couch."

I like the one about the psychiatrist who has two mail baskets on his desk—one marked OUTGOING—the other INHIBITED.

Nobody's immune from troubles. I know a psychiatrist who's

ready to flip. Every morning his wife comes down to the office and keeps rearranging the couch.

People have the strangest jobs these days. I know a guy who's a psychiatrist in a watch repair shop. Psychoanalyzes cuckoo clocks.

I won't say they're emotionally disturbed—but this is the first couple in history with a sleep-in psychiatrist.

Mental problems can hit you at any age. Why I just read of an eighty-year-old man who went to a psychiatrist. It seems he's always chasing women—but he can't remember why.

Isn't that sad about the TV cowboy who's going to a psychiatrist? At the end of every show he has to kiss his horse—and lately, he's been looking forward to it.

He's one of those Navy psychiatrists. No couches—hammocks!

PSYCHOANALYSIS: where you can spend more on a couch than some people do on a six-room house.

PRACTICAL PSYCHOLOGY: putting a hard, lumpy mattress in the guest room.

I know a promising young psychiatrist who had to give up the business. Just couldn't keep from going: "Tch, tch, tch, tch!"

Is he a good psychiatrist? He's brilliant! Pioneered the Miltown-Fiscal method of treatment. Gives his patients a tranquilizer ten minutes before presenting the bill. . . . You see people going bankrupt with smiles on their faces. . . .

It's like I was telling her psychiatrist the other day. I said: "Doc, I don't care if she thinks she's an octopus, but it's costing me a fortune in elbow-length gloves!"

You think you've got troubles. I know a fella who's been going to a psychiatrist for five years. Just found out the guy's deaf!

The latest thing in psychiatry is group therapy. Instead of couches, they use bunk beds.

So this woman goes to a psychiatrist and complains that her husband thinks he's Barry Goldwater. The headshrinker says:

"What's so wrong with that? At least it shows he's interested in bettering himself." She says: "I don't mind that, Doc—it's hearing that Inaugural Address, over and over again!"

I'm a little concerned about my brother 'cause he thinks he's a Russian Wolfhound. *Now* he thinks he's a Russian Wolfhound. He *used* to think he was a St. Bernard—up to the time he lost his liquor license.

To give you an idea what kind of a psychiatrist he is—for three years he treated a patient who felt he was always on the outside, looking in. Then he found out the guy was a window cleaner.

Then there's the woman who introduced her psychiatrist to her hubby. She said: "Doc, I want you to meet my husband—one of the men I've been telling you about."

I once knew a psychiatrist who couldn't get served in bars. They claimed he was too Jung.

Once upon a time there was an ambitious psychiatrist who became so skilled, so successful, so famous—all the world beat a psychopath to his door.

Did you hear the one about the psychiatrist who ushered out his last patient for the day, heaved a weary sigh of relief, locked his desk, turned on his hearing aid, and went home?

R

REDUCING

If you really want to lose weight, don't keep your bathroom scale in the bathroom. Put it in front of the refrigerator.

I won't say I'm getting fat—but every summer it's frightening how that hammock seems to sag a little more.

I just blended a reducing tablet with a sleeping pill. It's for people who want to take light naps.

He operates a reducing salon in Wall Street—for stocky brokers.

The whole country's going diet crazy! Did you hear the latest? Lump saccharine for overweight horses.

One diet preparation claims it's the only one that works—all the rest are wishful shrinking.

Wouldn't it be awful if the makers of all those 900 calorie drinks were misogynists—and the stuff was really concentrated malted milk?

I understand Metrecal is starting its own TV show. They'll call it the Metrecal Movie of the Week and it'll show such all-time favorites as: THE THIN MAN . . . CHARGE OF THE LIGHT BRIGADE . . . THE GENERAL DIETS AT DAWN , . . THE INCREDIBLE SHRINKING MAN. It'll be a blast!

I like the one about the pastry shop that put a sign in front of its eclairs: HELP STAMP OUT METRECAL!

She's really a wonderful girl. 18 going on 19. 200 pounds going on Metrecal.

A little song dedicated to all you women on diets: METRECALI ROSE.

And for all you girls in the audience who have been trying to lose weight—I've got a very simple diet for you. You eat all you want of everything you like—steaks, spaghetti, French fries, cake —and you can eat as many times a day as you like—only you can't use a knife and fork—chopsticks. . . . Guaranteed to lose you five pounds a week if your name isn't Wong. . . .

Did you hear the one about the reducing salon that advertises: REAR TODAY—GONE TOMORROW?

Or the reducing salon that started a weight-losing contest—with the winner getting the Nobelly Award?

DIETS: for people who are thick and tired of it.

RELIGION

To all our Jewish friends we wish a Happy New Year! I'll bet it's a few months before you stop putting 5726 on letters.

Next month we have another great holy day—Yom Kippur, the Day of Atonement. Or, as a rabbi once defined it to a Christian audience, Instant Lent.

I just thought of a wonderful thing to give up for Lent—my New Year's Resolutions!

I'll tell you how serious that feud is—even Minneapolis ministers don't mention St. Paul.

And now we take you to the Garden of Eden where a fig leaf is slowly wafting down from a tree. Eve looks up and says: "Look, Adam, look! The Invisible Man!"

ATHEIST: a guy who doesn't care who wins the Notre Dame—SMU game.

Then there's the missionary cannibals couldn't boil. He was a friar.

One tribe of African cannibals is so impressed with the missionary sent them, they've completely changed their way of life. Now on Fridays they eat nothing but fishermen.

Did you hear about the Yogi who had a terrible nightmare? Dreamed he was completely surrounded by navels—and all of them were contemplating him!

Or, the missionary who was captured by cannibals and just as they were about to kill him, he held up a cigarette lighter, flicked it, and a bright dancing flame popped up. The natives were awe-stricken and released him on the spot. "It's a miracle!" cried the chief. "That's the first time I've ever known a lighter to work the very first time!"

RESORTS

Let's face it, you can't please everybody. Like the resort in Monticello that wanted to vary its program, so it brought up the entire 106-piece New York Philharmonic, the full Metropolitan Opera Company, and 40 featured dancers from the Russian Ballet. It was a night to remember. Dancing, singing, rapturous music, spectacle! When it was all over, the manager came out beaming from ear to ear and asked the guests if they enjoyed it. One guy stood up and he could hardly contain his annoyance: "So what happened to Myron Cohen?"

I've been in wealthy resorts but nothing like this. I mean—it's all right to have money but who wears mink babushkas?

The management has asked me to make this announcement: PLEASE DON'T SMOKE IN BED. BUSINESS MAY BE GOOD BUT WE STILL DON'T HAVE GUESTS TO BURN.

I've got an idea for a summer resort that's gonna make a fortune. We don't book acts from New York—unmarried doctors!

What a resort! Their motto is: WHERE THE TURF MEETS THE SURF. I got news. It should be: WHERE THE DEBRIS MEETS THE SEA.

The management has asked me to make this special announcement. For the balance of the season, please be extra careful when using the pool. The lifeguard didn't get his raise.

147

How 'bout that sun up here? My eyes haven't been so red and tired since I lived across the street from the YWCA. . . . But it's so healthy. Really, I've never seen such healthy girls by the pool. Some of them look like they're having a permanent surplus sale. . . .

What a resort. After two days I got snow-blind from looking at sour cream.

It's just wonderful being up here in (NAME OF RESORT). All day long we feed ourselves and all night long we feed the mosquitoes.

Have you ever seen a menu like they have up here? Seven different appetizers; six different soups; 14 entrees; 28 desserts; Sanka, Postum, coffee, tea, cocoa, milk, brandies, cordials. Then that really inspired touch—the relish tray filled with Bromo-Seltzer, Alka-Seltzer, Brioschi, Tums, bicarbonate and your choice of stomach pumps.

This happens to be one of the biggest clubs in the mountains. If you don't believe me—see those people at the far end of the bar? Take a look when they pay the check. Canadian money!

It's incredible how one resort tries to outdo the other. Last week one place enlarged its dining room by 400 seats. Right away the hotel next door enlarged its dining room by 900 seats. Hadda take out the kitchen to do it but—

Our impression of a Catskill resort at two in the morning:
C: (BANGS ON THE MIKE HEAD) You got a girl in that room?
S: Yeah!
C: (EFFEMINATELY) Oh, you traitor!

RESTAURANTS

I guess you heard about that new restaurant downtown—the _____? I understand prices are so high, sometimes it takes *two* credit cards to pay the check.

It's one thing to be economical, but this is the only restaurant in town that uses a substitute for margarine!

THE JOKE-TELLER'S HANDBOOK

TELEPHONES

Ten years ago, did you ever think you'd be reading in bed by the light of the telephone? . . . It's little! It's lovely! It lights! It's polite—it only speaks when spoken to! . . .

My daughter was on the phone last night and it must have been something important. Lasted three Cokes and an apple. . . . I get to use the phone once a month—when I call up to say: "Our bill couldn't be *that* high!" . . .

And the telephone company is starting a new public relations program. Coming out with a special rate for the clergy—parson to parson.

He's the type who worries about odd things. Like—if you put a telephone in your car—what directory do they list it in?

I don't know what this world is coming to. This morning I'm driving into town and I see this Model T Ford trying to pass a block long chauffeured Lincoln Continental. And this car had everything! Air-conditioning, tiger skins on the floor, a millionaire sipping a Martini and listening to a hi-fi set. Suddenly there's a ringing noise and the millionaire picks up a telephone in the Lincoln, listens a moment—then lowers a power window, hands the receiver out to the guy in the Model T, and says: "It's for you!"

There's a telephone operator in Chinatown who's all shook up. Keeps getting Wong numbers.

TELEVISION

B: I'll make you a star! I'll put you in nightclubs, theatres, movies, not to mention television!
G: Television?
B: I told you not to mention television!

I just read about a TV producer who was doing fine with a summer replacement—until his wife found out about her.

It's one of the world's great unsolved mysteries—like where do elephants go to die—and where do summer re-runs go the rest of the year?

I'm a little worried about television. The good guys win out on every program but the 11 O'CLOCK NEWS.

I'll tell you how dull television is getting. Kids are doing their homework again!

To get on television, they say you gotta keep trying. And he is! He's made more pilots than a stewardess.

So these two vultures are flying over Don Knotts. One nudges the other and says: "Looks like someone beat us to it."

It doesn't make sense. Like the Canadian TV station that hired a 40-28-36 model as a weather forecaster; put her in a low-cut gown; then had her talk about cold fronts. They had to let her go. Nobody believed her!

Everyone's so title conscious these days. I know one fella who calls himself a TV psychiatrist. You should call him when your set breaks down.

I know a couple who wanted to buy a color TV set but they couldn't afford it. So they bought a Cadillac instead.

I don't care what the manufacturers say, those color TV sets still need improvement. Like last year, I saw the Kentucky Derby on one. I won't say what it looked like, but most of the race the horses stood still and the color ran.

You can't resist progress. I just read where there are now 5,000,-000 color TV sets in the United States—100,000 in homes and the rest in showrooms!

Now the big thing is TV TOOTHPASTE. It comes in a colored, 21-inch tube.

TV SET: a machine with a picture in front; tubes in the middle; and an installment behind.

A recent survey shows that most families now own two television sets. So I want to thank all you people for letting me come into your bedroom too.

At our house, I'm happy to say, we despise television. In fact, some nights we sit up till two in the morning—glaring at it.

Thirty years ago, people thought television was impossible! Some still do.

What a horrible way to die—run through by a portable TV antenna.

MINUTE MAN: a guy who can make it to the refrigerator, fix a sandwich and a short beer, and be back before the commercial's over.

I put a TV set in my car—it almost killed me and it's not what you think. Here I am buzzing along at 80 miles an hour watching Ed Sullivan . . . comes a commercial, I get out to go to the bathroom. . . .

Isn't television wonderful? To be able to sit in the comfort of your own home; take off your shoes; drink beer; eat potato chips; and all night long watch your wife's favorite programs—that's living!

Television has brought about some interesting side effects. I'll bet we're the only country in the world with more cockroaches in the living room than in the kitchen.

Oh, man, am I pooped! I told my wife, I can't go on like this. Somebody's gotta fix that remote control for the TV set!

Have you been to the antique shop that specializes in 7″-TV sets?

I'll tell you how old this TV set is. On Tuesday nights I see Milton Berle running around in women's clothes!

I just love watching those old movies on television. Like last night, I saw one so old—Bing Crosby was carrying a comb.

I don't know what's happening to television. For years you watched old movies. Now it's getting even worse. During the summer you watch old TV shows. . . . I saw one so old, it featured 30 minutes of snow, ghosts and blur—with selected short test patterns. . . . I don't mind the drama repeats so much. It's those re-runs of last year's 11 o'clock news that get to me! . . .

Did you see that old Tarzan picture on Channel 9 last night? All about these elephants who travel hundreds of miles over mountains, through jungles, across rivers—just to be able to die in the elephants' graveyard? And I finally figured out what kills them—the trip!

I just saw one of those real old gangster pictures on TV. You know the kind—where it shows the robbers driving up to a bank—and finding a parking space right in front.

It's bad enough they show old American pictures on television—now they're starting to show old English pictures. I saw one so old, Henry the Eighth was played by Henry the Ninth!

Did you see that picture on television? THE SON OF THE INVISIBLE MAN? There's a kid with problems. Wants to follow in his father's footsteps but he just can't find them!

I got an idea that's gonna bring back quiz shows. Really! You're given the question *and* the answer—but you gotta guess who sent it in.

Next week they're presenting an epic of the television industry entitled WHAT MAKES SAMMY RE-RUN? or IS THE LATE SHOW LATE ENOUGH?

It's the latest thing. TV Breakfasts for people who watch the Late Late Late Late Show.

Daytime TV—sometimes known as the reason why a woman's work is never done.

We owe a lot to daytime television. Why if it weren't for daytime television, think of all those millions of women who might otherwise be out—driving!

Have you ever watched those educational TV shows on Sunday? I did last week and an astronomer was saying that other galaxies are pulling away from us at the rate of a thousand miles a second! A thousand miles a second! And all I could think of was: "Maybe they know something!"

And there's no question that TV is educational. I don't think there's one of my kids who couldn't rob a stage, dry-gulch a sheriff, or rustle some cattle.

But you gotta give television credit. Twenty years ago, kids were out in the streets—exposed to all kinds of criminals, perverts, violence, temptation! Isn't it wonderful that now they can be exposed to all those things—right in the safety of their own living rooms?

TEXAS

They really do things big down in Texas. They've got an auto showroom in Dallas, three acres wide and wall-to-wall with Cadillacs, Lincolns, Imperials. And over in one corner, there's this little pile of Volkswagens with a placard: TAKE ONE.

I know one Texan who's so rich he doesn't even have his Cadillac air-conditioned. Just keeps a half-dozen cold ones in the freezer.

I won't say the kids are spoiled, but one of them just gave his mother a Cadillac for her birthday. Saved half his allowance for six weeks.

My idea of real living is that big Texas family with six sports cars to run around the ranch in. Twice a year, they send the foreman out in a Cadillac to round them up.

These antique car clubs are really catching on. They just formed a new one down in Texas. It's restricted to people whose Cadillacs are no longer under the new car guarantee.

Did you hear the one about the Mother Goose book they published in Texas? And all the kids are reciting: "The Butcher, The Baker, The Cadillac Maker."

I don't wanna sound envious, but I think some of those Texans spoil their kids. It's all right to give nice Christmas presents but who ever heard of a chauffeur-driven kiddie car?

I love that new car accessory they're selling down in Texas. It's a combination safety and money belt.

It's such a thrill driving from Fort Worth to Dallas. Where else can you see money belts drying on the line?

You can always tell who the nouveaux riches Texans are. They're the ones who wear their money belts *outside* their shirts.

Last night one of those Texas oilmen walked in and checked his hat. So the girl said: "Would you like to leave your attaché case, too?" He said: "What attaché case—that's my wallet!"

He's one Texan who hasn't forgotten where all the money came from. All his furniture is oily American.

One of those Texas oilmen is giving his son a whole cowboy outfit for Christmas: a ten-gallon hat; pearl-handled six-guns; 3,000 head of cattle and Lorne Greene.

I'm almost afraid to tell you about the rich Texan who gave his son a chemistry outfit for Christmas—DuPont!

Have you heard about the lazy Texan who bought his wife a yacht for Christmas—so he wouldn't have anything to wrap?

Did you hear about the pregnant housewife in Texas who got an overpowering craving for mints? So her husband bought her Fort Knox?

Or the rich Texan who bought his dog a little boy?

I know a Texan so rich, he bought a bomb shelter with a built-in house!

A crook walked into a Texas bank, pointed a gun at the teller and growled: "Gimme $20,000 and I want it in small bills—50s, 100s, and 500s."

I admire that Texas oilman who's donating $60,000,000 to further one of the greatest concepts of our time. Yes, he's taken it out of petty cash . . . and they're starting work on it next Monday. Gonna air-condition Texas! . . . And man, that's a lot of hot air to overcome. . . .

I dunno about those Texans. Last week I was showing one of them around New York. I pointed out the Empire State Building, this fantastic edifice—and he said: "Son, I got news for you. Down in Texas, I've got an outhouse that's bigger'n that!" And I'll tell you something. I believe him. He'd need it!

It's one of those Texas bathrooms—where the sink has three taps —hot, cold, and bourbon.

Talk about success stories, they tell the one about the poor Texas housewife (whaaa?) who wanted to brighten up her home but she couldn't afford new curtains. So she decided to dye the old ones red. She got a big washtub, filled it with a bright red dye, went to get the curtains—when a little lamb came scampering in, tripped over the tub and landed kerplunk—right in the middle of the dye. Two days later, a passing New York tourist saw the red lamb, thought it was a rare new species, and bought it for five times the going rate. So the woman thought it over, bought another lamb, dyed it red—and sold it to another tourist for five times what it was worth. Before long, she was in mass production —turning out and selling red lambs by the thousands. And would you believe it, today that woman is the biggest lamb dyer in Texas!

A highly unreliable source informs us of the fella who dies, goes to Heaven, and is strolling down the streets of gold, listening to the angelic music—when suddenly he sees a column of men, trudging along in chains. Shocked to the core, he runs to St. Peter and asks: "Prisoners? In Heaven?" And St. Peter nods his head sadly and answers: "Texans. They keep trying to get back!"

THANKSGIVING

Thanksgiving—the day everyone is thankful with the exception of those who are on a diet.

Every year around Thanksgiving and Christmas you see such helpful articles on HOW TO CARVE A TURKEY—and they're really practical. Now if I can only find a butcher who sells those turkeys with the dotted lines on them.

I like the one about the rich kids in a private school putting on a Thanksgiving play—all about the pilgrims sailing for Plymouth Rock. One of the kids just had a bit part. He's the one who wired ahead for reservations.

Sure you've got things to be thankful for. If nothing else, be glad you're not a turkey!

That's the trouble with American Thanksgiving dinners. You eat one and two days later you're hungry again.

I'm working on something that'll revolutionize the poultry world. Turkeys crossed with kangaroos. It'll be the first turkey in history you can stuff from the outside!

Here it is almost Christmas and we're still working on our Thanksgiving turkey. And I mean we've had every leftover combination known to mortal man. Have you ever tried turkey a la mode? . . . Turkey with sweet and sour sauce? . . . Turkey pizza, there's a good one! . . . Turkey on the half-shell. . . . For lunch I got a turkey sandwich. No bread. One slice of dark meat between two slices of white meat. . . . I don't know whether I'm gaining weight or growing a wattle. . . .

TIPPING

People are so easy to shake up. If you don't believe it, next time you pay at a toll bridge—leave a tip.

Everybody's tip-happy down there. I'm buying a newspaper and I dropped the nickel. A bellboy picked it up—hadda give him a quarter tip!

S: I live, man! Why I eat in a different restaurant every day!
C: I don't tip either.

I don't know what this world is coming to. Yesterday I saw a guy drive into a three-minute car wash—and toss the crew a dollar to hurry it up!

I must say this about the Superintendent of my building. This man stops in regularly to see if everything's all right. Hasn't missed a Christmas.

But Christmas is getting so commercial. Last week I got a Christmas card from the elevator operator and I've been so busy, I didn't get a chance to give him anything. This morning I got another card: "Season's Greetings from the Elevator Operator— SECOND NOTICE!"

TRAVEL

You gotta be on your guard these days. I know a guy who signed up for a SEE AMERICA FIRST TOUR—and it cost him $4,000. Went to San Juan, Fairbanks, Nome, and Honolulu!

I once knew a spinster who went on a world cruise. I don't know what she did, but every time she sees one of those labels: MADE IN JAPAN—she just smiles.

If you really wanna get shook up, eat in a Chinese restaurant in Quebec. Where else can you find fortune cookies printed in French?

It's incredible the number of striptease clubs in Paris today. You'd think the French would know better than to make sex a spectator sport.

I know a guy who never came back from one of those European tours. Got into a street fight in Venice.

Isn't that a wonderful name for a place—the No-tel Motel?

I've been doing some sight-seeing. Went out to the Art Museum to look at the Rembrandts. What a genius this man was! Can you imagine what he could have done if he had numbers to follow?

Everything's so expensive. I just got back from Rome. No more three coins in the fountain—bills!

Italy is fantastic! Why, Naples took my breath away. Capri captured my soul. Rome stole my heart away. And Florence! Flo got me for $300 worth of travelers checks.

The San Francisco Tourist Association has been trying to create events to interest visitors. Like next Sunday they're having a Cable Car Drag Race. . . . And I'm sure it will be. . . .

I spent the summer in Jerusalem. Flew with that new outfit, Biblical Airlines. . . . I got a little worried when I saw their planes—BC8s. . . . I don't know whether that's a model number or the year they were built in. . . . No motors, just four ravens with the passengers saying: "Nevermore, nevermore!" . . .

I have the same feeling about taking my wife to Paris as I have about taking my car downtown. The big problem is where to park it.

Parisians have a saying—the naughtiest thing you can see in Paris is an American tourist.

East Berlin is an incredible city. Looks like they tore down parking lots to put up old tenements.

Everybody's becoming education-conscious in Germany. The optimists are learning English; the pessimists are learning Russian—and the realists are learning Swedish.

UNDERTAKERS

Did you hear the one about the undertaker who closes all his letters with "Eventually yours?"

Someone just told me there's a mortuary out in California with their own radio show—15 minutes of dead air.

Isn't that a wonderful slogan for a crematorium? WE'RE HOT FOR YOUR BODY!

It doesn't make sense—like an undertaker running a 1¢ sale.

I don't know what the newspapers are coming to. Did you see the Classified Section of the _____ this morning? 1946 HEARSE FOR SALE. BODY IN GOOD CONDITION.

I love the one about the two hippies who open a funeral parlor—and out front they put a big sign: IF YOU'RE REAL GONE—WE DIG YOU THE MOST! . . . They've even developed a philosophical viewpoint. They figure death is nature's way of telling you to slow down. . . .

UNEMPLOYMENT

This happens to be the anniversary of Calvin Coolidge's classic insight into the world of economics: "When a great many people are out of work—unemployment results."

I won't say he's a bum. Let's just say he suffers from chronic unemployment.

Congress is trying to extend unemployment insurance. Pretty soon you'll be able to get paid for a whole year without working.

Yes, God helps those who help themselves—and Washington those who don't.

I've got an idea that's gonna make me a fortune. It's a club for people collecting unemployment insurance. The dues are 50¢ a week—and if they find you a job—we fight the case!

UNIONS

The unions are pushing for a four-day week but there's one thing that bothers me. Who's gonna pay for the two coffee breaks and lunch hour I'll be missing?

Unions are getting such a bad name, it's no wonder they're called Brother Hoods.

Remember the good old days—when the only strikes the country had were silver and gold?

People are never satisfied. For years we've been looking forward to automation. Now it's finally here and everybody's worried. One union got so scared it went out on strike—for shorter machines and longer hours!

UNITED NATIONS

The UN is trying to get all the nations in the world to live as one big family. And if the family is anything like mine—they've succeeded.

You hear some amazing titles at the UN. For instance, Switzerland doesn't have any navy but they have a Minister of the Navy. Which is pretty crazy until you learn of the Russian Minister of Justice.

I hope they settle this trouble between the two Chinas soon. I tell you, I'm getting so tired of these domestic litchi nuts!

V

VACATIONS

Here it is, vacation time again. You know what a vacation is. That's what you take when you can no longer take what you've been taking all along.

Vacations are sure educational—no doubt about it. Like spending two weeks in a Volkswagen with the ones you thought you loved most.

You know what I can't understand about vacations? How you can throw your wife and kids in the car—along with two relatives, half the household furniture, and three parakeets—then tell the neighbors you're gonna get away from it all.

And you can always tell it's vacation time by the Highway Department. That's when they close up all the regular roads and open up all the detours.

And for all you long-distance vacation drivers, we're making up special signs for the front of your cars. The letters'll be two feet high, fit right over the grille, and say: ATTENTION DEER! MOTORIST CROSSING!

Isn't this a wonderful place to spend a vacation? And the people! Did you ever meet such an attractive, intelligent, poised, alert bunch of phonies in your life?

I won't say the room is small but twice a day I have to go outside to let my mosquito bites swell.

Watch out for those summer romances, girls. Remember, the only thing you can trust in pants is a lamb chop!

It's vacation time again. Two weeks devoted to finding places you should stay away from next year.

My idea of a person who's had a real vacation is the guy who can come back to town and hear (CURRENT HIT RECORD) for the first time.

All you people who spent your vacations in Paris—don't you think they ought to call it the Rue de la Paix and Paix and Paix and Paix?

We had a wonderful vacation. Went through London, Paris, Rome, and $6,000.

I just figured out why there are so few marriages in July and August. With everybody away on vacation, the office collection'd be too small.

You can tell that vacation time is here. Yesterday I was on a bus —and there must have been 110 girls in there with me—on the way to the beach. I mean, it was crowded something wonderful!

This year, why not spend your vacation at home? Show your neighbors you're unusual—creative—home-loving—strapped!

W

WAR

Can't you just see the leader turning to his general staff and saying: "This could be the end of civilization as we know it!" Then he fires the first bow and arrow at the enemy.

The Pacifists have finally adopted a positive approach. Instead of banning the atom bomb, they're trying to bring back poison gas.

I think it's ridiculous to talk about World War III. I mean, we just couldn't afford to win another war.

There's one thing about a World War III. At least we won't have to worry about veterans' benefits.

A hundred years ago, when a soldier retired, he hung his long rifle over the mantelpiece. I wonder what soldiers nowadays are gonna do with their push buttons?

Two sailors were castaway on a desert island during the war. For 13 years they lived a hermit's existence—never seeing a ship, an animal, or another human being. And then after 13 years, they looked out across the water—and there, floating in on the tide, was a bottle! One of those giant-size Coca-Cola bottles! They splashed out into the surf, scooped it up—and then a look of unspeakable horror crept over their faces. One turned to the other and gasped: "Sam! Sam, we've shrunk!"

They say the next war may only last seven or eight hours. Which is really wonderful if you stop to think about it. We'll still have our evening free.

Personally, I think we oughta do something about the Defense Department. If there's ever another war—it'd be nice to have the Army, Navy and Air Force all on one side.

After the show we're all gonna get up and do the WORLD WAR

III CHA CHA. It's just like the WORLD WAR II CHA CHA only with different partners.

If you stop to think about it, Moses probably had the *first* summit meeting.

Wouldn't it be funny if we fought our next war over disarmament?

GEORGE WASHINGTON

Washington's Birthday is celebrated in every state except Texas. Down there, they figure any man who couldn't tell a lie, isn't worth remembering.

It wasn't easy for Washington to be elected the first President of the United States. Just think—he couldn't complain about the mess in Washington.

February is a very important month in American history. Lincoln proved you can be born in humble surroundings and still become President of the United States. And Washington—he proved that being rich is no handicap either!

February—the month we salute Washington. First in War; First in Peace—and last in the American League!

I can't understand it. People like Richard Burton, Noel Coward, Peter Ustinov come over here and they're so charming, so witty, so brilliant—I keep wondering why George Washington couldn't get along with the British.

They say George Washington never told a lie. Today he would have been first in war; first in peace; and last to make it in politics.

WASHINGTON, D.C.

Don't you think it's a little embarrassing to be President of the United States? All your neighbors know what you do; where you go; what you make.

So much is happening in the world. The President must be afraid to walk into his office in the morning and ask: "What's new?"

I wanna know when the President is gonna deal with the biggest surplus problem of them all—bigger than wheat; bigger than corn; bigger than butter—wire coat hangers!

Personally, I think we ask too much of the President of the United States. It isn't bad enough all those crucial decisions he has to make; the crushing responsibility; the never-ending stress and strain—but in addition to all this, he has to go out and root for the Washington Senators!

I've been reading about those Congressmen who get their work done—family style. . . . I know one Senator who's got the only office in Washington with wall-to-wall relatives. . . . Pays his son $7,000 a year to act as administrative assistant; research analyst and technological adviser—and the marvelous part of it is—the kid's only twelve! . . . months! . . .

Have you tried the new Senatorial Cocktail? Three and you wind up speaking from the floor.

I know a guy who wants to raise all congressional salaries to $200,000 a year! That way, they'll all be in the highest bracket—and a lot more interested in cutting taxes.

Rome had Senators. Now I know why it declined. (WILL ROGERS.)

I never get too upset over the things they say in Washington—'cause I finally figured it out. The way I see it, Washington, D.C., doesn't have a bona fide village idiot. And so the residents shouldn't feel deprived, the Senators all get together—and each day, one of them takes a turn at it.

SING: Old man river. That old man river. He don't say nuthin', he don't do nuthin'! (COMMENT) Sounds like a Jr. Congressman.

Congress is getting eager to adjourn—which comes as a surprise to me. I'd have thought they'd be afraid to go home.

Tonight's show is dedicated to America's greatest single factor for world peace—Congressional Junkets! . . . Let's face it, we just can't drop a bomb on Moscow. We'd kill more Congressmen than Communists! . . .

There's enough hot air coming out of Washington to blow up every plastic wading pool in the country!

The way everybody's running around in Washington, it's as if somebody pressed the panic button and it got stuck!

The Democrats are holding another one of those $100 a plate political dinners. $100 a plate! I wouldn't even pay my dentist that much!

Every year thousands of people go down to Washington to see the government in action—and every year it's getting harder to tell whether that's one word or two.

WEALTH

Rich? This boy doesn't count his money; he measures it.

Rich? This boy could retire and live off the interest on the interest.

Loaded? He's got bills in his wallet with pictures of Presidents I never even heard of. . . . Like Chester A. Arthur. . . . There's a wild one—a $24,000 bill. It's for people who buy Rolls-Royces. . . . And the $105 bill for hundred-dollar call girls who observe the city sales tax. . . .

Loaded? This is the only kid in town with a Cadillac tricycle.

Loaded? These people have Jaguars the way our kitchen has mice.

It's all right to have money but don't you think a four-room Cadillac is a bit ostentatious?

It's all right to show people you've got money—but a Cadillac with stained glass windows?

This town is so rich, the station wagons are bigger than the station.

Rich? This man has a split-level Jaguar!

With him, money is no object. Yesterday we went for a drive and stopped for gas. The attendant said: "Regular or High Test?" He said: "What Regular or High Test? Gimme the best—Homogenized!"

It's wonderful to have money. Everything becomes so simple—even the parking problem. You just buy cheap cars and leave 'em.

There's no question he's rich—but don't you think it's a little ostentatious—going to a drive-in movie in a taxi?

It's one of those exclusive towns. Other places have Little League baseball. They have Little League polo.

C: This boy is so rich, he flys his own two-engine plane!
S: Big deal! A lot of people fly their own two-engine planes.
C: In their living room?

C: Money brings its own problems. Why I know a very rich family and they're all in a snit because the son is dating one of the servants.
S: What's so awful about that?
C: It's the butler.

I really shouldn't talk to him like that 'cause this boy is lousy with money. Of course, he's lousy without money too.

Lavish? The rugs in one room are so thick, you need snowshoes to get to the piano.

Did you read where Liberace had a sequinned dinner jacket made up that cost him $3,000? Isn't that ridiculous? Why anyone who pays more than $2,000 for a dinner jacket is just plain crazy.

So, this chorus girl married an elderly playboy with $10,000,000 —and all her friends mailed her GET WILL cards.

As one deer said to the other: "Man, I wish I had his doe!"

Well, that's the way it goes. As J. Paul Getty puts it—another day, another $42,653!

There's only one trouble with living in the lap of luxury. You can never tell when luxury is gonna stand up!

WESTERNS

It's what you might call an adult, modern, sophisticated Western. It doesn't take place in Dodge City—but in a suburban shopping center three miles out.

Personally, I think they're overdoing this adult Western stuff. I saw a movie last night and I swear—the corner saloon was a member of the Diner's Club.

It's one of those modern Westerns—where the hero couldn't get the badmen in any other way—so he jailed them for income tax evasion.

I was watching this Western on TV last night—and the villain was so mean, so ornery—every time the hero had something to say—he stood in front of the Teleprompter!

I kept track last week and there were 328 outlaws, bandits, cattle rustlers and all-round no-good varmints killed on TV Westerns. If this keeps up, I'm going to start my own series—FRONTIER MORTICIAN!

Isn't it fascinating how many twists they keep coming up with on Westerns? Like that new one: HY BRACKETT—FRONTIER BUSINESS-MAN. . . . In the very first scene he plugs the villain; his latest record; and a diner on Route 66. . . .

Talk about unusual Westerns, I just saw one written, produced, directed and acted by Indians. It's the only Western on TV in which the cavalry *doesn't* arrive in time!

It's one of those real psychological Westerns. The Indians don't say: "How!" They keep saying: "Why?"

Would you believe it, there are 37 different Westerns on TV right now! Thirty-seven! Wouldn't it be funny if the Indians demanded equal time?

I know an inventor who's working on a top secret project for TV. Crossing a horse with a kangaroo—for cowboys who want to ride inside during cold weather.

It took years but I finally saw a realistic Western on TV. The doctor was saying: "You shot bad, Tex?"—and the cowboy looked up and said: "Doc, you ever knowed anybody who was shot good?"

You turn on one of those Westerns and everybody's so tense, so edgy, so ready to fly off the handle. And you'd be the same way if *your* pants were that tight!

I was watching Bonanza last week—and they had a badman on that show that was so tough, so ornery, so quick on the draw—they had to call in marshals from three other channels to whup him.

Fast? This boy could stand in front of a full-length mirror and beat himself to the draw!

I know a guy who is making a fortune out of TV Westerns. Sells calamine lotion to cowboys with itchy trigger fingers.

One sheriff is so tough, if he joined a nudist colony, he'd wear his star anyway!

I know one TV cowboy who's losing his show this week. Seems like he rounded up more posses than sponsors.

I know a girl who's making a fortune in Westerns. Measures .45 —.22—.38!

I'll bet that two years from now most of those TV Westerns'll be nothing more than a memory. Just a flash in the panhandle.

Remember the good old days—when Western heroes shot off their guns instead of their mouths?

Those TV Westerns are wonderful. I saw one last night that was so old—the wide-open, hell-raising, Western frontier town was Cleveland. . . . It was one of those Westerns you couldn't even call adult. Senile—that's what I think it was. . . .

I won't say how old this Western was—but it gave me a chance to look at something I've never seen before—Gabby Hayes' chin!

And those Westerns never die. I saw one so old, Billy the Kid was played by Billy the Kid.

WIVES

The Duchess of Windsor claims sex might eventually become another bit of household drudgery. I wonder if husbands will come up with the same solution? Have a girl come in once a week to help out?

And now a special message to all you wives in the audience: Girls! Have you been feeling unloved? Don't. Think of Solomon's 500th wife.

She's such a loving wife. Every time I go away on a trip, she keeps a light burning in the window. And every time I come back does she have a surprise for me! An electric bill for $300!

Talk about an exciting weekend, yesterday my wife and I were standing in front of a wishing well—and she fell in! I didn't realize those things worked!

The first person who invents a wife-sized garbage can is gonna make a fortune.

This may come as a shock to you people—but I've got only three weeks left to live. Then my wife comes back from the country.

Talk about bad luck—once I had money, a luxurious apartment, the love of a beautiful woman—then my wife had to walk in and louse up everything.

What have I got to complain about? I've got a secretary who slits open my letters in the office—and a wife who steams them open at home.

This morning she fired my secretary. Claimed she was a security risk—hers.

It's bad enough my wife criticizes me—but my mother-in-law criticizes me too. I'll bet I'm getting the only stereophonic nagging in town!

I've been feeling depressed all day. You see, on May 14th, 1946, I decided to murder my wife. Then my lawyer tells me I'd get twenty years. And all day long I've been thinking: "So—today I'd be free!"

Things like Valentine's Day mean something to me. I always try to do a little more for my wife—like holding open the door when she goes out on her paper route.

I can't understand her. She says she refuses to work now that we're married. I said: "Kid, get a hold of yourself. If it's good enough for Queen Elizabeth, it's good enough for you!"

Do you realize there are over 20,000,000 working wives in this country? I mean, daytime TV can't be *that* bad!

WOMEN (AGE)

I didn't realize she was too young for me until I started to talk about rumble seats—and she didn't know what they were.

You know what a memory expert is. That's any woman who's just learned another woman's age.

My wife is 34 years old and she's still going through a change of voice. Like she'll be yelling at me and screaming and ranting and raving. Suddenly the phone rings—maple syrup!

Now is that a nice thing to say—after all we've meant to each other? Remember when we took that solemn vow that we'd grow old together? Then you went ahead without me?

Her face was so wrinkled, she didn't dare wear long earrings. Made her look like a Venetian blind.

She's very sensitive about her age. I understand even the government sends her social security check in a plain envelope.

WOMEN (APPEARANCE)

My wife was a little upset this morning. Her living bra tried to commit suicide. . . . Claimed it was leading an empty life. . . . I don't wanna be catty—but the only thing a low-cut gown does for her is show off her pearls.

I got a wonderful idea for a business—the Foreign Aid Falsie Company—specializing in aid for underdeveloped areas!

He's made a very unusual job for himself. Goes door to door selling falsies. Sort of a Fuller Bust man.

Some girls put on a sweater and look sexy, vivacious, alluring! She puts on a sweater and looks like Mort Sahl.

I won't say the kid's underprivileged—but she'd have to wear falsies to look flat-chested.

I once went out with a blind date. I was told she was 38-25-35—and she was, but not in that order.

I was reading about this agency that specializes in ugly photographers' models. Calls them the Unretouchables.

WHEN A GIRL MAKES HER EXIT WITH A WIGGLE: You know, we haven't had Jell-O in a long time.

Presenting: STELLA HOUSTON—the real life story of one woman's fight against girdle creep-up.

My wife'd be a beatnik right now if it wasn't for one thing—can't find a leotard size 46!

Life gets so monotonous. I've got a secretary who's getting a little behind at work—and a wife who's getting a big one at home.

She's got a very unusual figure: 25-32-148. It isn't so much a figure as a puddle.

HINDSIGHT: what a woman should have before wearing slacks.

C: I've been having a lot of trouble with my wife. I got her a present last week and she can't fit into it.
S: So bring it back and get a larger dress.
C: What dress? It's a Volkswagen!

It's all right to watch television—but 14 hours a day? . . . And it's beginning to affect her. She's the only woman on the block with square eyeballs! . . . Talk about fixed stares—when the CBS eye looks at her—it blinks! . . .

You might say she had an early American face. Looked just like George Washington.

And those bags under her eyes! What can I say? Her nose looked like it was wearing a saddle.

Did you hear the one about the girl who read Exodus and was so impressed, she had her nose changed back?

Now the big thing is white lipstick and white powder. Six months ago we had girls; now they all look like Camille on a bad day. . . . Which proves an old contention of mine. If one idiot wears something, it's ridiculous. If enough idiots wear it, it's chic! . . .

Now she's getting a double chin. I think it was just too much work for one.

She calls herself a straight actress. I didn't believe it until I saw her measurements—36-36-36.

I won't say she's built like a truck—but I notice nobody ever passes her on the right.

You've seen the way models walk—so calm, so relaxed, so poised? Well she's got her own style altogether—moves like a turtle with ingrown toenails.

Isn't she something? Looks like a Den Mother for beatniks.

It's one of life's great tribulations. Every time I meet a girl who can cook like my mother—she looks like my father.

TO BEAUTIFUL GIRL: Aren't you too young to be trusted with a figure like that?

It's the kind of a figure that gets the once-over twice.

B: They tell me when you were eight you were just a little butterball.
G: That's right.
B: Well you sure melted nice!

Isn't she wonderful? She reminds me of a deck of cards. A little mixed up but stacked!

B: Tell me, how do you keep such a ravishing figure?
G: Well to be perfectly honest, I don't really pay much attention to it.
B: Man, you don't know what you're missing!

WOMEN (CHARACTER)

Talk about arguments, if her lovin' was as hot as her temper—WOW!

Life is full of contradictions. Take the girl who walks back from a car ride. I'll bet she gets a lot hotter than the one who doesn't.

I won't say what she does for a living but they threw her out of one hotel 'cause she didn't have a permit for a parade.

It doesn't take much to soften her up. You just have to soak her in money.

There once was a girl
Who had a little curl
Right in the middle of her forehead;
When she was good
She was very, very good,
And when she was bad—
She always slept till eleven the following morning and had a tremendous appetite for breakfast.

Experienced? She's had more hands on her than a doorknob.

Innocent? This girl could be a test pilot for chastity belts.

It's the story of a poor but honest 20-year-old girl who won't marry an 80-year-old millionaire because of the difference in their urges—ages.

She's such a composed, dignified sort of girl. One day we were having dinner when she leaned over and in a very genteel way said: "Pardon me, but I don't believe your hand and my leg have been introduced."

A member of the 400 got a little tipsy on sherry and confessed she had been born in Bismarck, North Dakota. And, suddenly realizing her faux pas, added: "Of course, I was conceived in Newport!"

But she's a lady. You can tell by the way she holds her pinky up while chomping on a pork chop.

I like the one about the girl who sent her boy friend a rush telegram: BUY THREE RINGS FAST. ENGAGEMENT, WEDDING AND TEETHING. HAVE I GOT NEWS FOR YOU!

She's lovely! She's engaged! She uses friends!

I wouldn't call her promiscuous. Let's just say she's a dish that happens to appear on a lot of different Menus.

I call my wife SAC. She's always up in the air about something.

My wife suffers in silence louder than anyone I know.

I mean, I believe in women having rights—but I haven't worked the controls on our electric blanket since the honeymoon.

I won't say she's narrow-minded—but if it gets any worse, she'll only have to use one earring.

My wife always does something sentimental for Easter. Like last year she gave me a rabbit punch.

My wife's such a doll. Last Valentine's Day she sent me a card and signed it: "Guess who—and you'd better!"

Togetherness, to me, is my wife leaning over me while I'm watching the Friday Night Fights, and asking: "What inning is it, dear?" . . . And I tell her the seventh; and give her a score; and she goes back to her reading—content in the knowledge that she's making this marriage work. . . .

WOMEN (CLOTHES)

She's always complaining she's got nothing to wear. Friends—her clothes closet is packed so tight—there are moths in there that still haven't learned how to fly.

The calendar may call it Easter Sunday—but to women all over the country, it's Decoration Day.

This hat had so many flowers on it, three funerals followed her home.

And girls—I've got a question I'd like to ask you about those pointed shoes. If you happen to have more than one toe, what do you do with them?

You know what I like? Those dresses you see ballerinas wearing. You know the ones—the long stiff skirts with the curb feelers.

Never mind the shortage of teachers. The greatest threat to a well-informed America is the new short skirts. I haven't read a paper on a bus in months!

Dresses are getting so short it's embarrassing—and in the winter, a problem. I know three girls suffering from chapped hips!

I'll never forget the first time she wore a muu muu. Did you ever see a crowd in a shroud?

Did you hear the one about the two hippies watching the Lady Godiva pageant in Coventry, England? One turned his bulging eyes to the other and said: "Man, what stable's that chick riding for?" And the other answered: "I dunno, but dig those crazy silks!"

I guess you read about that new bra called the BIRD DOG? It makes pointers out of setters.

And so, as the Maiden Form said to the hat: "You go on a head— I'm gonna give these two a lift!"

I gave her something we both can enjoy—a sweater.

Kind of a funny thing happened at the Greyhound Company last week. A woman called up and said she found a brassiere on one of the seats. The operator said: "Really? What bus?" And the woman answered: "38B!"

It's the sad story of a girl who bought herself a Ship-and-Shore blouse—and then discovered she didn't have the coastline for it.

I just saw a testimonial by ——————— who claims she wears a living bra. Man, if I had a job like that, I'd be living too!

TOPLESS BATHING SUIT: You know, her mother'd be furious if she ever saw her in that outfit. It's hers.

It's incredible how styles have changed. Fifty years ago women wore bathing suits down to their ankles. Then they wore them down to their knees. Five years ago it was down to their hips. I just got back from the Riviera and they don't even wear them down to the water.

I don't know what she's up here for but I know it isn't for sports. She's got three bathing suits and the labels all say DRY CLEAN ONLY.

You should see the Bikinis they're wearing at the beaches this year. We've got more sun-kissed navels than California!

Now I know why they call those bathing suits Bikinis. They don't cover the girls atoll.

I can remember when girls who went to the beach only peeled *after* they got sunburned.

It must be wonderful to be a girl in the summertime. Just think. They can either go to the mountains and see the scenery—or go to the seashore and *be* the scenery.

As a gag I once gave her one of those old-fashioned bathing suits with the covered knees and long skirt—and to make it even more unusual, it was made of corduroy. She was just delighted with it —laughing, skipping, running around, whirring up a storm! Then she jumped in the water and we never saw her again.

Talk about a wardrobe, did you notice that stole she had on? I don't wanna say what she paid for it, but that girl is wearing a Cadillac around her neck!

I know a chorus girl who got a mink coat and spent the next six weeks describing it to her friends and explaining it to her parents.

You can be sure of one thing when a girl gets a mink coat. She's either gonna look beautiful or guilty.

You hear the darndest things while walking to the elevator. I passed one room and a girl was saying: "Take back your mink, sir. I'm not that kind of girl!" And he said: "What kind are you?" And she said: "Size 16. If you'd just take it in a little around the waist and shorten the sleeves—."

Have you noticed that stole she's wearing? It's the latest thing— wash and wear mink.

Isn't she lovely? And so kind to animals. Why that girl'd do anything for a mink.

I just went by the checkroom and I've never seen so many minks and sables and silver foxes. Looks like Zsa Zsa Gabor's closet.

This is a fur coat? Looks like an old army blanket with five o'clock shadow.

WOMEN (DRIVING)

What can I tell you? She's the type who makes men climb mountains, swim rivers, lose their minds—a woman driver!

She may not be a good driver, but when it comes to parking, this girl can do a bang-up job!

And to any man teaching his wife how to drive—remember—the first 100 gears are the hardest!

Can this girl drive! Gets 22 miles to a fender!

Yesterday she came in and said: "I don't wanna upset you but I scratched the left rear fender a little." I said: "Oh?" She said: "Yes. If you want to look at it, it's in the trunk."

You should have heard one of the kids screaming this morning—all because Mommy backed the car over her doll. I said: "Don't come crying to me. I told you not to leave it on the porch!"

I won't say she's rough on a car, but this is the first time in history Chevrolet ever asked for its guarantee back.

But I've got to admit she's an imaginative driver. Who can get a ticket for making a U turn in the Lincoln Tunnel?

WOMEN (HAIR)

Women will do anything to be different. I'll bet in Sweden you'll find brunettes with blonde roots.

As Confucius once said: "Blonde who go to hairdresser once a month, soon show true colors!"

She's the all-girl showgirl type. The kind of a blonde gentlemen preferred even before she became a blonde.

Isn't she lovely tonight? And her hair—my favorite shade of peroxide!

Isn't that a wonderful hair style? Looks like a beanie with a fringe.

Vain? Every night she brushes her hair one hundred strokes. For five years now—every night—one hundred strokes! Her hair doesn't look any better but you oughta see the muscles in her arms!

My wife came home with one of those colored wigs they're wearing. I wouldn't let her in the house. I told her I'd love her when her hair was silver—but not tangerine!

You've never seen a more exotic-looking group of girls. One of them has a purple hair-do. And what makes it even more exotic —it's natural!

Which brings us to our thought for the day: Some of the ugliest rumors start in beauty shops!

WOMEN (WEIGHT)

She calls it a sylph-like figure and I don't give her an argument. Who's to say there's no such a thing as a big fat sylph?

She claims she's still got a schoolgirl figure and I believe her. The trick is to find it under all that fat.

I won't say she's fat—but who else has trouble getting into a bath-robe?

Then there's the girl who's three feet tall, weighs 250 pounds, and people keep inviting her to parties—especially if they need a hassock.

I won't say she's fat—she's just living beyond her seams.

Figures don't lie—but girdles sometimes redistribute the truth.

Isn't she sweet? I love every bone in her corset!